PERSONALISM

PERSONALISM

by

EMMANUEL MOUNIER

ROUTLEDGE & KEGAN PAUL LTD
Broadway House, 68-74 Carter Lane
London

LE PERSONNALISME
First published in France 1950

PERSONALISM
Translated by Philip Mairet
First published in England in 1952 by
Routledge & Kegan Paul Ltd
Broadway House, 68-74, Carter Lane
London E.C.4
Printed in Great Britain
by C. Tinling & Co Ltd
Liverpool, London, and Prescot

CONTENTS

v

CONTENTS

INFORMAL INTRODUCTION TO THE
PERSONAL UNIVERSE

THE word 'personalism' is of recent usage. Employed in 1903 by Renouvier to describe his philosophy, it then fell into disuse. Several Americans have made use of it, following Walt Whitman in his *Democratic Vistas* (1867). It reappeared towards 1930 in France, a very different climate of thought, to designate the first researches of the review *Esprit* and of some neighbouring groups (*Ordre Nouveau* and others) concerning the political and spiritual crisis then arising in Europe.[1] Laland's *Vocabulaire philosophe* gives the word currency in the 5th Edition of 1947. Contrary to all custom, the *Larousse* makes it a synonym for egocentricity. It follows, apparently, an undecided and branching course, that of an inspiration seeking and testing its directions.

However, what is called personalism today is by no means a novelty. The universe of the person is the universe of man. It would indeed be surprising if we had had to wait till the XXth century for its exploration, albeit under other names. The most recent personalism is grafted, as we shall see, upon a long tradition.

Personalism is not a system

Personalism is a philosophy, it is not merely an attitude. It is a philosophy but not a system.

[1] *Esprit* was founded in 1932: see its files and E. MOUNIER: *Manifeste au service du Personnalisme* (Aubier 1936); *Qu'est-ce que le personnalisme?* (Eduard du Seuil 1947). Upon a particular aspect: *Personnalisme catholique* (*Esprit*, Feb., Mar., April 1940), reprinted in *Liberté sous conditions* (Ed. du Seuil 1947).

Not that it fears systematization. For order is necessary in thinking: concepts, logic, schemes of unification are not only of use to fix and communicate a thought which would otherwise dissolve into obscure and isolated intuitions; they are instruments of discovery as well as of exposition.[1] Since it defines certain positions, personalism is a philosophy and not only an attitude.

But its central affirmation being the existence of free and creative persons, it introduces into the heart of its constructions a principle of unpredictability which excludes any desire for a definitive system. Nothing can be more profoundly repugnant to it than the taste, so common today, for an apparatus of thought and action functioning like an automatic distributor of solutions and instructions; a barrier to research; an insurance against disquiet, ordeal and risk. Moreover, a movement of original reflection should not be too quick to tie up the sheaf of its findings.

Also, though we speak, for convenience, of personalism, we ought rather to say that there is a plurality of personalisms and to respect their diverse procedures.

A Christian personalism and an agnostic personalism, for instance, differ even in their intimate disposition.

They would gain nothing by trying to unite in a middle way. Nevertheless they confirm one another in certain realms of thought, in certain fundamental affirmations and upon certain lines of practical conduct concerning individual or collective order; and that is sufficient to justify their use of the same name.

General Idea of the Personalist universe

One might expect that personalism would begin by defining the person. But one can only define objects exterior to man, such as can be put under observation. Here is my neighbour. He has a unique feeling of his body which I cannot have; but

[1] J. LACROIX: *Système et existence* (*Vie Intellectuelle* June 1946).

I can look at this body from without, examine its dispositions, its heredity, its form, its maladies; in short, I can treat it as an object of physiological, medical or other knowledge. He exercises functions, and there is a functional order and a functional psychology which I can *apply* to the study of his case, although they are not *he*, the whole man in his total reality. Moreover, and in the same way, he is *a* Frenchman, *a* bourgeois, *a* socialist, *a* catholic etc. But he is not *a* Bernard Chartier, he is Bernard Chartier. The thousand ways in which I can distinguish him, as *an* example of a class may help me to understand him, and above all to make use of him, they show me how practically to behave towards him. But these are merely sections taken, in each case, through one aspect of his existence. A thousand photographs put together will not amount to a man who walks, thinks and wills. It is a mistake to believe that personalism only means that, instead of treating men according to type, we take their shades of difference into account. Huxley's 'Brave New World' is one in which armies of doctors and psychologists are engaged in a re-conditioning of each and every individual based on detailed investigations. Since they do this from the outside and by compulsion, reducing all men to nothing but well-mounted machines in good working order, their super-individualized world is nevertheless the opposite of a personal universe, for everything in it is contrived, nothing is created and no one engages in the adventure of responsible liberty.

There are not, then, stones, trees, animals—and persons, the last being like mobile trees or a more astute kind of animals. The person is not the most marvellous object in the world, nor anything else that we can know from the outside. It is the one reality that we know, and that we are at the same time fashioning, from within. Present everywhere, it is *given* nowhere.

We do not, however, relegate it to the ineffable. A fount of experience, springing into the world, it expresses itself by an incessant creation of situations, life-patterns and institutions. But the essence of the person, being indefinable, is never exhausted by its expression, nor subjected to anything by which it is conditioned. Nor is it definable as some internal substratum, as a substance lurking underneath our attitudes, an abstract principle of our overt behaviour: that would still be a mode of being objective, the ghost of an object. It is the living activity of self-creation, of communication and of attachment, that grasps and knows itself, in the act, as the *movement* of *becoming personal*. To this experience no one can be conditioned nor compelled.

Those who carry it to the heights, call thence to all those around and below them. Their call awakens the sleepers, and as one responds to another, all mankind is stirred out of its drowsy, vegetative slumber. Whoever refuses to hear that call and will not enter into the experience of the personal life loses the feeling for it, as the sensitivity of an organ can become atrophied by disuse. He will then dismiss the idea as a mere complication of the mind, or as the mania of a sect.

There are, then, two ways of expressing the general idea of personalism.

One can proceed from the study of the objective universe, to show that the personal mode of existing is the highest form of existence, and that the evolution of pre-human nature converges upon the creative moment at which this achievement of the universe is attained. One may say that its central reality is this act of personalisation; the impersonal realities, or those that are more or less depersonalized (matter, living species and the ideas) being only the effects of a loss of speed, of nature's lagging-behind upon the road to personalization. The insect that mimics the branch, in order that it may be overlooked in its vegetative immobility, prefigures the man who buries himself in conventionalities rather than answer for himself; or the man who gives himself up to abstract ideas or sentimental effusions to escape the confrontation of events or other men.

But such a description, in so far as it is objective, can but imperfectly convey a reality which is not primarily objective.

Or one may openly live the experiment of personal life, hoping to convert to it a number of others who still live like trees, like animals or like machines. Bergson called for 'the appeal of the hero and the saint'. But these words must not deceive us: the personal appeal may spring from the humblest levels of human life.

This brings us to the central paradox of personal existence. The personal is the mode of existence proper to man. Nevertheless it has ceaselessly to be attained: consciousness itself can but gradually disengage itself from the mineral, the plant and the animal that weigh it down.

The history of the person, therefore, runs parallel with that of personalism. It will not unfold itself on the plane of consciousness alone, but throughout the length and breadth of the human struggle to humanize humanity.

Brief history of the notion of the person and of the personal condition[1]

To consider Europe alone, the sense of the person remains embryonic throughout antiquity until the dawn of the Christian era. The man of antiquity is absorbed in the city and the family, subservient to a destiny that is blind, nameless and stronger than the gods themselves. Slavery does not shock the foremost spirits of those days. The philosophers value only impersonal thought and its static order, which is the order of nature as well as of ideas. To them the singular appears as a blemish, whether in nature or in consciousness. Plato is tempted to reduce the individual soul to a participation in nature plus a participation in the city; whence his 'communism'. And for him as for Socrates, individual immortality is only a beautiful, bold hypo-

---

[1] Some indications concerning this history will be found in J. PLAQUEVANT: *Individu et personne, Esquisse des notions* (*Esprit*, Jan. 1938). Two histories of personalism are in preparation, in France and in the U.S.A.

thesis. Aristotle indeed declares that there is no reality except the individual; but his God cannot will with a particular will, nor can he know essence in the singular, nor love with a selective love. For Plotinus there lies, so to speak, a primordial fault at the root of every individuality, and there is no salvation but in a desperate flight back to the One and the Timeless.

Nevertheless, the Greeks had a keen sense of the dignity of the human being, which periodically brought troubles upon their impassible order. Their taste for hospitality and their cult of the dead in themselves bear witness of this. Sophocles tried, once at least (in *Oedipus Colonnus*) to replace the idea of blind Fate by that of a divine justice endowed with discernment. Antigone affirms that the witness of the eternal is against the powers. In *The Trojan Women* the notion of the inevitability of war is opposed by that of the responsibility of men. Socrates searches the utilitarian arguments of the sophists with the probe of irony, and upsets his interlocutor by putting the latter himself in question as well as his knowledge. His 'Know thyself' is the first great personalist revolution of which we know. But this could have only a limited effect against the surrounding resistances. Finally, we must not forget the Sage of the *Nichomachean Ethics*, nor the Stoics and their moving presentiment of the *caritas generis humani*.

It is *Christianity* that, first of all, imports into these gropings a decisive notion of the person. We can hardly comprehend today what a complete scandal this was to the thought and sensibility of the Greeks.

(1) Whilst for them, multiplicity was an evil inadmissible to the spirit, Christianity made it into an absolute, by affirming the creation *ex nihilo*, and the eternal destiny, of each and every person. The supreme Being which through love brings them into existence no longer makes the world a unity through the abstraction of the idea, but by an infinite capacity for the indefinite multiplication of these separate acts of love. Far from

being an imperfection, this multiplicity, proceeding from super-abundance, bears that superabundance in itself as an illimitable interchange of love. Long was this scandal of the multiplicity of souls to vex whatever survived of the sensibility of the ancient world; and Averroes was again to feel, in his time, a need to imagine one common soul for the whole human race.

(2) The individual human being is not a crossroads where several participations in general realities meet (matter, ideas etc.) but an indissoluble whole, of which the unity is prior to the multiplicity because it is rooted in the absolute.

(3) It is not the abstract tyranny of a Destiny, nor of a heaven of ideas, nor is it an Impersonal Thought indifferent to their individual destinies that reigns over persons. It is a God who is himself personal, albeit in an eminent degree; a God who has 'given himself' to take on and transfigure the condition of mankind, one who offers to each person a relation of unique intimacy, of participation in his divinity; a God who affirms himself not at all, as contemporary atheism has supposed (Bakunin, Feuerbach), by what he takes away from man, but by granting man a freedom analogous to his own, by his readiness to be generous to the generous.

(4) The profound purpose of human existence is not to assimilate itself to the abstract generality of Nature or of the Ideas, but to change 'the heart of its heart', ($\mu\epsilon\tau\alpha\nu\omega\alpha$) there to introduce, and thence to radiate over the world, a trans-figured Kingdom. The secrecy of the heart, in which this trans-mutation of the universe is decided by personal choice, is the inviolable domain which no one can judge and of which nobody knows, not even the angels, but God alone.

(5) To this transformation man is freely called. Liberty is constitutive of his existence as a creature. God could have created immediately a creature as perfect as a creature can be, but he preferred to invite man freely to develop his humanity and the purpose of the divine life. The ability to sin, that is, to refuse his destiny, is essential to the full exercise of liberty.

Far from being a scandal, it is the absence of this that would alienate man from God.

(6) This absoluteness of the person neither cuts him off from the world nor from other men. The Incarnation confirms the unity of earth and heaven, of the flesh and the spirit, as soon as the redemptive value of human work has been assumed by grace. The unity of the human race is for the first time fully affirmed and doubly confirmed: every person is created in the image of God, every person is called to the formation of one immense Body, mystical and physical, in the charity of Christ. The collective history of humanity, of which the Greeks had no idea, now makes sense and even has cosmic meaning. Even the conception of the Trinity, emerging from two centuries of controversy, produces the astounding idea of a Supreme Being which is an intimate dialogue between persons, and is of its very essence the negation of solitude.

This vision was too new, too radical, for all that it implied to be known at once. History, of which it is the seed and essence in Christian eyes, is to develop its meanings until the end of history.

Long and obstinately, throughout the medieval period, it is opposed by all that persists of the social and political ideas of Greek antiquity. It takes several centuries to pass from the spiritual rehabilitation of the slave to his effectual liberation: we have not yet inferred from the equality of souls the equality of social opportunity: the spirit does not move faster than the body. The pre-technical conditions of the feudal epoch prevent the liberation of medieval humanity from excessive servitude to labour or from hunger; and hence prevent the construction of a civic unity over and above social classes. The dualistic temptation, although Christianity has from the first fought strenuously against it, is a continuing factor in social sensibility down to our own age. At the height of the Middle Ages it maintained the long Platonic aberration that hampered full re-affirmation, by the Albertino-Thomist realism, of the dignity of matter and the unity of the human being. The notion of the person had, it is true, been elucidated little by little throughout the trinitarian and Christological controversies from the second to the sixth centuries; it was more and more richly harmonised by the Greek sensibility, although the Roman juridical spirit, which lent precision to its formulations, was at bottom resistant to it. Each great thinker added some new touch; but the logical and conceptual machinery inherited from the Greeks, rooted in classification and generalization, did not facilitate its expression.

Modern rationalism and idealism, with their dissolution of concrete existence in the idea, are now commonly traced to *Descartes*. This, however, overlooks the decisive character of the *Cogito* and its complex implications. The act of a subject no less than the intuition of an intelligence, this *Cogito* is the affirmation of a being breaking the interminable tram-lines of the idea and asserting itself with authority as existent. Voluntarist thinkers, from Occam to Luther, have prepared the way. Thenceforth philosophy is no longer a lesson to be learnt, as by force of habit it had become in the scholastic decadence, but a personal meditation which anyone is invited to begin again on his own account. It begins, like Socratic thinking, with conversion—conversion to existence.[1] At the same moment, the rising bourgeoisie are breaking the oppressive forms of the feudal structure. But the bourgeoisie, in reaction against a too cumbrous society, exalt the isolated individual and are the founders of the economic and spiritual individualism that is still rampant among us. Similarly, Descartes bequeaths to us, in his *Cogito*, the germs of the idealism and metaphysical solipsism which are so deeply to undermine classical personalism from Leibnitz to Kant, abundant as are the riches it will distribute on its way.

[1] Maxime Chastaing: *Descartes, introducteur à la vie personelle* (*Esprit*, July 1937).

Hegel remains the imposing and monstrous architect of the imperialism of the impersonal idea; in which all things and all beings are dissolved into their representations: it is not by chance that Hegel comes, in the final reckoning, to believe in complete subservience of the individual to the State. Yet we ought not to forget how much personalism owes to *Leibnitz* and to *Kant*, or what the dialectic of personality owes to the whole reflective effort of idealist thought. *Pascal*, the father of dialectic and of the modern existential consciousness, would be the greatest master of them, if Jansenist doctrines had not side-tracked him towards the lofty and solitary religion which was also to ensnare Kierkegaard. Nor, by the way, should we ignore *Malebranche* and his *Traité de Morale*; or *Rousseau*, working to death the impoverished rationalism of the Enlightenment, misled by individualism, but yet giving back to his century the feeling for solitude and laying foundations for the education of the personal self. Let us also recognise the importance of *Goethe*, seeking in 'the deed' the dynamic unity of spirit and matter. But of the XIXth century we have to underline three names which do not attain their splendour until the century following, so little can they breathe in the ideological climate of their own.

Maine de Biran is the latest of the fore-runners of French personalism. He denounces the mechanical mentality of the ideologues, who resolve all concrete existence into the pseudo 'elements' of thought, and he looks for the self in the propulsive effort by which man acts upon the world. At once an inner initiative and a muscular initiative, this experience discloses, in the centre of every consciousness, its relations with the exterior and objective: we may not therefore set consciousness and space in opposition; all consciousness is spatialising, it affirms itself in space. Maine de Biran's thinking is a remarkable elucidation of the roots of personality and of its sphere of expansion.

Kierkegaard, for his part, confronting the 'System' as re-

presented by Hegel and his spiritualist imitators, maintains
the irreducibility of the source and spring of liberty. A prophet
of the paradoxical and dramatic greatness of man, in conflict
with the optimism of bourgeois comfort and facile sophistry,
but unhappily caught in the romantic drift of the time,
Kierkegaard becomes unable, in his lofty solitude, to rejoin
the world and mankind. But upon the brink of an epoch that is
descending to any servility for the sake of a sort of vegetative
well-being, he carries almost to paroxysm his defence of the
sense of freedom, and its rootedness in the sense of the absolute.

Like Kierkegaard, *Marx* reproaches Hegel for having made
the spirit of abstraction, and not the actual man, the subject
of history; for having reduced the living reality of men to
the Idea. In his view this falsification corresponds to that of
the capitalist world, which treats the labouring and producing man as an object in history, thus expelling him from
himself, as it were, and from his natural realm at the same time.
What one might call the Socratic revolution of the XIXth
century, the fight against all those modern forces that tend to
depersonalise man, thus appears to divide into two branches:
the one, as in Kierkegaard, appeals to modern man, dazzled
by the discovery and exploitation of the world, to remember
his subjectivity and his liberty; the other, following Marx,
denounces the mystifications into which man has been inveigled
by social constructions derived from his material conditions,
and reminds him that his destiny is not only in his heart but
in his hands. Disastrous division! Thenceforth the two lines
cannot but diverge; and the task before our present century is,
perhaps, not to seek to reunite them where they can never
again meet, but to rise above their divergence towards the harmony that they have banished.

Beneath these searchlights whence radiate the great illu-
minations of the century, we have to follow the tardy soci-
ological development of human conditions. With whatever
reserves one may regard the French Revolution, it marks an

important phase of social and political liberation, limited though it is in its context of individualism. But thenceforth things develop with a kind of fatality. On the one hand individualism, finding a congenial climate in the period of capitalistic triumph, flourishes beyond all bounds. The liberal State is its crystallisation into codes and institutions, but whilst that State professes a personalism that is ethical (of a Kantian colour) and political (in the bourgeois style) it leaves the urban masses in material conditions of slavery—social, economic and, before long, political. Romanticism heightens the passion of the individual at every level of affectivity but, in the isolation which it accentuates, it leaves him no choice except between the desperation of solitude and the dissipations of desire. Recoiling before this new peril, and fearing the imprudences of desire, the petty-bourgeois world suppresses both under an upholstery of mediocre satisfactions; it establishes the régime of precautionary individualism. Meanwhile the rapid proliferation of techniques breaks the frontiers of the individual and his restricted circles, opening-up wide spaces and collective relationships on every hand. Bewildered individualism takes fright, equally from the anarchy into which it is sinking and from the collectivism by which it is menaced. It tends to justify its own rear-guard operations as the 'defence of the person'. *Renouvier* was already denouncing the passion for metaphysic and the political quest of unification. But the 'person', for him, is above all negation, refusal to associate; it is the liberty to oppose; to doubt, to offer resistance both to mental intoxication and, correlatively, to every form of collective affirmation whether theological or socialistic. What a healthy reaction against certain dangers, and yet how likely to lead one into anarchic temptations! Such temptations sterilised, in part, the great work of *Proudhon*. The impassioned anarchy of *Nietzsche* dramatizes this hazard, but encourages the same tense attitude of negation, which reappears today in certain forms of existentialism.

Nevertheless the choice is not between a blind impersonalism, an enormous cancer that proliferates till it kills, and the proud despair which prefers merely to be annihilated standing up. There are men who have begun to dispel these monstrous terrors by developing a richer notion of the personality of man, of his relations with the world and with his works. After *Lotze*, the first translations of *Max Scheler* and of *Buber* are contemporary with the first books of *Berdyaev*, writers who refuse consent to the sacrifice of either spiritual freedom or technique, just as *Bergson*, a little earlier, would renounce neither the well-spring of liberty nor the rigour of the sciences. After *Laberthonnière*, *Maurice Blondel* defines a dialectic of spirit and action which has badly upset all the scenery of the abstractionists. Whilst *Péguy* gave lyrical expression to all the themes that we are about to unfold, *Jacques Maritain* has been applying the clarifying realism of St. Thomas to the most immediate of contemporary problems. *Gabriel Marcel* and *Jaspers*, the one Christian, the other agnostic, are also contributors of capital importance to the structural description of the personal universe. P. L. Landsberg places himself very close to them in his unfinished work. Upon these more definitely personalist researches, and their continuation in the review *Esprit* since 1932, the *existentialist* revival and the *Marxian* revival exert two lateral pressures. The former has very largely contributed to the reanimation of personalist problems: the latter is stirring up the whole world of contemporary thought to extricate itself from idealist mystification, to enter into the common predicament of mankind, and to relate the highest philosophy to the problems of the modern city. One might thus distinguish an existentialist tangent of personalism (comprising Berdyaev, Landsberg, Ricoeur, Nédoncelle), a Marxian tangent often concurrent with this one, and another tangent, more classical, in the French philosophic tradition (Lachièse-Rey, Nabert, La Senne, Madinier, J. Lacroix).

Outside of France, movements that claim to be personalist

are appearing in several places, and others that do not profess personalism are akin to it. In England, the name is appropriated by one or two reviews and by the *Personalist Group* of J. B. Coates. They have been inspired primarily by John Macmurray, John Middleton Murry, N. Berdyaev and Buber; and one ought not to forget Newman. A context of religious subjectivism, of political liberalism and of Ruskinian anti-technicism (H. Read) has sometimes led them rather far from the line of French personalism; but the dialogue is proceeding. In Holland the personalist movement, born in a camp of war-hostages in 1941, developed only upon the political plane and endeavoured to realise a new socialism through the "Mouvement Populaire Néerlandais", which came to power at the liberation before its fusion with the socialist party. In the United States a strong current of thought is developing, associated with the names of Royce and Howinson, the Fathers Bownes, Brightman and Flewelling. In Switzerland, where they have not forgotten Secrétan, there is the publication *Cahiers Suisse Esprit*. Groups of a kindred inspiration are being formed in the countries liberated from Fascism.

$$\star \qquad \star \qquad \star$$

Since the person is not an object that can be separated and inspected, but is a centre of re-orientation of the objective universe, we shall now have to turn our analysis upon the universe that it reveals, in order to elucidate its structures upon different levels. Of these we must never forget that they are only different angles of vision on the same reality; the truth of each depends upon its relation to the others.

PART ONE

THE STRUCTURE
OF
THE PERSONAL UNIVERSE

CHAPTER I

EMBODIED EXISTENCE

MODERN philosophies of spirit divide man and the world between two independent series, material and spiritual. Sometimes they accept, as brute fact, the independence of the two series (psycho-physical parallelism) abandoning matter to its determinism, whilst safeguarding the absolute right of the spirit to legislate within its own domain: the connection between the two worlds then remains unexplained. Sometimes they deny any reality to the material world, to the point of making it a mere reflection of the spirit: the importance of such an apparent world then becomes somewhat of a paradox.

Such schema are rejected from the start by personalist realism.

The person immersed in nature

Man is a body in the same degree that he is a spirit, wholly body and wholly spirit. His most fundamental instincts, eating and reproduction, he has elaborated into the subtle arts of gastronomy and courtship. Yet the great philosopher is attacked by headaches, and St. John of the Cross used to vomit during his ecstasies. My moods and my ideas are shaped by the climate, by geography, by my situation upon the crust of the earth, by my heredity and perhaps beyond all this by unfathomable currents of cosmic rays. Into these influences the supervening psychological and collective determinants are interwoven; there is nothing in me that is not mingled with the earth and the blood. Research has shown us that the great religions spread along the same routes as the great epidemics. Why should we be shocked at this? Missionaries also go on legs, and have to follow the contours of the landscape.

So much for the truth, and it is considerable, of the materialist analysis. But it is nothing new. The indissoluble union of the soul and the body is the pivot of Christian thinking. It does not oppose 'spirit' to 'the body' or to 'matter' in the modern acceptation of the terms. In Christianity the 'spirit'—in the composite meaning of modern spiritualism, which signifies at once the thought ($\nu o u s$) the soul ($\psi \nu \chi \acute{\eta}$) and the breath of life—is fused with the body in existence. When both together strive in the direction opposed to the supernatural vocation of man, Christianity calls this movement 'the flesh', and means by that the downward drag of the soul as much as of the body; when it strives towards God, body and soul together collaborate with the power of the spirit ($\Pi \nu \epsilon \hat{u} \mu a$) in the substantial kingdom of God and not in some ethereal realm of spirit. Though original sin has wounded human nature, it is the composite man in his totality who is stricken; and ever since the time of the Gospels the malice and the perversities of the spirit have attracted more anathemas than those of the flesh in the narrower sense of the word. The Christian who speaks of the body or of matter with contempt does so against his own most central tradition. According to mediaeval theology, we cannot normally attain to the highest spiritual realities or to God himself except by thwarting matter, and by the force we exert against it. But in truth this is the Greek contempt for the material, that has been transmitted from century to century down to our own days, under false Christian credentials.

We have today to overcome this dualism in our way of life as in our thinking. Man is a natural being: by his body he is a part of nature, and the body is everywhere with him: we must now consider what this implies.

Nature—exterior, pre-human, unconscious psychological nature, including impersonal involvement in society—is not

4

the human evil; man's incarnation is not a fall. But since it is the ground of the impersonal and the objective, it is an abiding *occasion* of perversity. Poverty, like abundance, can undo us. Man is beleaguered as it were between the one and the other. Marxism is right in thinking that the ending of material poverty is the ending of an aberration, and a necessary stage to the development of humanity. But it is not the ending of all aberration, even upon the natural plane.

The person transcends nature

Man is a natural being. But is he no more than that? Is he altogether a sport of nature? Or does he, plunged into and emerging out of nature, transcend it?

The difficulty is how rightly to think this notion of transcendence. Our minds resist the representation of a reality whose concrete existence is wholly immersed in another but which nevertheless exists on a higher plane. One cannot be on the ground floor and on the sixth story at the same time, as Léon Brunschvig said. But this is using a spatial image to ridicule an experience that is not imaginable in space. The universe is full of men going through the same motions in the same surroundings, but carrying within themselves, and projecting around them, universes as mutually remote as the constellations.

Then let us look at nature. Let us dismiss the materialist myth of an impersonal Being of Nature, with limitless powers. We will also dismiss the romantic myth of a benevolent Mother, sacrosanct and unchangeable, from whom one dare not separate oneself on pain of sacrilege and disaster: both of these myths subject active and personal man to an impersonal fiction. In truth, nature reveals nothing to our rational understanding but an infinitely tangled web of tendencies, and we cannot even tell whether this is reducible, beyond the systems we construct in order to grasp it, to any logical unity at all. By what authority are we ourselves to be reduced to such systems?— to Pavlov's chains of associated reflexes, for instance?

5

If we are to render an account of humanity, we must grasp the living reality of man in his total activity. Pavlov's experiments are artificial creations of the laboratory: their results present us with a mechanistic view because they isolate the subject under conditions that are in themselves wholly mechanical. The man escapes them. "Man is a natural being, but a natural human being,"[1] and the singularity of man is his dual capacity for breaking with nature. He alone knows the universe that enfolds him, and he alone transforms it—he, the most defenceless and the least powerful of the larger animals. What is infinitely more, man is capable of love. The Christian will add, that he is capable of co-operation with God. We must not ignore the salivary reflexes, but neither should we be obsessed by them.

The determinisms that surround us are indeed no idle word. But the notion of determinism, though it has not been dismissed from science as some imagine, is now limited to the description of large-scale material phenomena. Infra-atomic phenomena escape it; biological phenomena surpass it. At the sub-atomic level the physicist finds no more than a " pseudo-causality", which is such that "the same cause may produce one or another of several possible effects with only a certain probability that such-and-such an effect will be produced and not another." (L. de Broglie). Man is no longer cramped in a vice of determinism. Though we remain concretely involved in, and restricted by many determinisms, every new law that a scientist discovers adds another note to the gamut of our liberty. So long as the laws of aerodynamics remained unknown, men dreamed of flying: when their dream inserted itself into a system of necessities, they flew. Seven notes make but a restricted register; yet those seven notes have made musical invention possible for several centuries already. Whoever argues from necessities of nature to the denial of human potentialities is either bowing down before a myth or trying to justify his own fatalism.

[1] Marx: *Political Economy and Philosophy*

The emergence of creative personality can be read throughout the history of the world. It appears as a struggle between two contrary tendencies, of which one is *a constant trend towards depersonalization*. This is seen not only in matter itself, which indeed is impersonality, passivity and indifference, for it subsides into entropy (degradation of energy) and into sameness or repetition as its natural end. It attacks life, reduces its urge, degrades species to the monotonous repetition of the typical, makes discovery degenerate into automatism, curbs vital audacity within systems of security from which inventiveness disappears, prolongs many movements by inertia till they work against their own purpose. Finally, it lowers the tension of social life and the life of the spirit by the relaxations of habit, of routine, of generalized ideas, and of diurnal gossip.

The other tendency is the *movement of personalization*, which strictly speaking, begins only with man, though one may discern a preparation for it throughout the history of the universe.[1] The phenomena of radio-activity are already announcing a break in the rigid fatalities of matter. Henceforth life takes on the appearance of an accumulation of energy progressively organized into more and more complex nuclei of indeterminacy: a fan of possibilities is thus opened to the free choice of the individual, according to biological predisposition, for the formation of centres of personality. The atomic particle, emptied of all qualities, is no longer identifiable even by its position in space, since the quantum theory forbids us to accord it any precise or lasting localization. An embryonic individuality thus appears even in the atom itself, in the very structure of matter. In the animal, individuality attains to a clearer definition; although nature treats it with scant consideration, multiplying it with prodigality and expending it in massive waste. Two out of two million eggs of a fly hatch and grow into mature individuals. Animals know nothing of reflec-

[1] Concerning this preparation, see the writings of P. Teilhard de Chardin.

7

tive consciousness or of conscious reciprocity. The good of the individual is subordinated to that of the species whenever the two conflict. It is in the human person that this series of forms finds, not indeed its explanation but its significance.

The emergence of the personal universe does not arrest the course of natural history, but takes it up into the history of man, without wholly bending it thereto. We sometimes speak of 'primitive man' as if he were a being long lost in the mists of prehistory; but if we attained to the vivid and searching experience of personal reality, we should find our origins still very near to us. The worldly and moralistic comedy in which we play our parts is secretly designed by our instincts, our interests and our needs; even what we call the 'life of the spirit' devotes a great part of its activity to concealing these unacknowledged actors behind the arras of justification and prestige. Materialism is partly right, so long as it is historical and gives its references, though wrong in the realm of values. For at the stage which humanity has so far attained, and for the great majority, and except for the individual conversions which are always possible (that makes three restrictive conditions), our biological and economic situation still massively manages our behaviour. Numerous individuals and the great movements that some of them have inspired in ages past, doubtless ever since man became man, have broken out of this servitude; again and again, alone or in fellowship, man reaches by a leap the heights of humanity; but man in the mass continues, step by step, his earthbound way towards them. The personal universe does not yet exist except in individual or collective exceptions, in promises yet to be redeemed; yet its progressive conquest is the essential history of mankind.

The consequences of this condition

Certain important consequences follow from the condition we have just defined.

(1) It is pointless to approach either the science of 'matter'

or the science of 'spirit' with disparagements or idealizations that are ineffectual on the plane of reality.

(2) Personalism is not a kind of spiritual doctrine, but rather the reverse. It includes every human problem in the entire range of concrete human life, from the lowliest material conditions to the highest spiritual possibilities. The crusades were at one and the same time, and with differing degrees of justification in each case, outstanding expressions of religious sentiment and economic convulsions in a declining feudalism. It is therefore true that the explanation by instinct (Freud) and by economic analysis (Marx) are valid ways of approach to *all* human phenomena, including the highest. On the other hand none, not even the most elementary, can be understood apart from the values, the systems and the vicissitudes of that personal universe which is the immanent goal of every human spirit and of the whole travail of nature. Spiritual and moralist doctrines are impotent because they neglect biological and economic necessities; but materialism is no less futile for the opposite reason. As Marx himself said, 'abstract materialism' and 'abstract spiritualism' come to the same thing; it is not a case of choosing the one or the other, but 'the truth which unites them both' beyond their separation. More and more clearly, science and reflection are confronting us with a world that cannot do without man, and with man who cannot do without the world.

(3) We must apply to the plane of action what we have just said about the sphere of understanding. In every practical problem, the solution must be verified at the level of the biological and economic substructures, if the measures proposed for higher reasons are to be viable. Is this child abnormally idle or indolent? Examine his endocrines before you start lecturing him. Do the people grumble? Study their pay packets before denouncing their materialism. And if you want them to show more virtue, first give them that material security which you are passing on from father to son and without which—

9

as you may forget—your own social moderation might be less conspicuous.

Reciprocally, the biological or economic solution of a human problem, closely though it may conform to elementary needs, will be imperfect and precarious if it does not take account of the profounder aspirations of man. The spiritual, too, is a substructure. Psychological and spiritual maladjustments linked to an economic disorder may gradually undermine any solution achieved on the economic plane alone. And the most rational of economic systems, if it be established in disregard of the fundamental requirements of personality, bears within it the germs of its own decay.

Embodied Existence

Personalism thus opposes idealism, whenever idealism: (a) reduces all matter (and the body) to a reflection of the human spirit, absorbing it into itself by a purely mental activity; or (b) resolves the personal subject into a diagram of geometrical or intellectual relations, whence its presence is excluded; or (c) reduces it to a mere receiving-station for objective findings. For personalism, on the contrary:

(1) With however powerful and subtle a light the human mind may be able to penetrate the structure of the material universe, even to its most delicate articulations, materiality still exists, with an existence that is irreducible, autonomous, and opposed to consciousness. It cannot be resolved into relations internal to consciousness. That is the affirmation that Marx-Engels called 'materialist'. Yet it is in line with the most traditional realism, with a realism which does not refuse to assimilate the valuable findings of idealist criticism. What is alone radically foreign to consciousness is dispersion, pure, blind and unknowable. One cannot speak of any object, still less of a world, except in relation to a consciousness that perceives it. It is therefore useless to seek to reduce matter to a network of relations. What could we make of the relations that were

not perceived? The dialectical relation between matter and consciousness is as irreducible as is the existence of the one and of the other.

(2) I am a person from my most elementary existence upward, and my embodied existence, far from de-personalizing me, is a factor essential to my personal status. My body is not one object among others, nor even the nearest object—for how then could it be one with my experience as a subject? In fact the two experiences are not separate: *I exist subjectively, I exist bodily* are one and the same experience.[1] I cannot think without being and I cannot be without my body, which is my *exposition*—to myself, to the world, to everyone else: by its means alone can I escape from the solitude of a thinking that would be only thought about thought. By its refusal to leave me wholly transparent to myself, the body takes me constantly out of myself into the problems of the world and the struggles of mankind. By the solicitation of the senses it pushes me out into space, by growing old it acquaints me with duration, and by its death, it confronts me with eternity. We bear the weight of its bondage, but it is also the basis of all consciousness and of all spiritual life, the omnipresent mediator of the life of the spirit. In this sense, we may acknowledge with Marx that "a being which is not objective is not a being"—immediately adding, however, that a being which was nothing but objective would fall short of the full achievement of being, the personal life.

The personalization of nature

It is not enough for personality to conform to nature, out of which it proceeds, or to react against nature's provocations. The person turns against nature to transform it, progressively to subdue nature to the sovereignty of a personal universe.

Up to a point, personal consciousness affirms itself by simple

[1] This is the essential thesis of Gabriel Marcel and of Maine de Biran. See also G. Madinier: *Conscience et Mouvement*

acceptance of its natural environment. Recognition of the real is the first stage in all creative life; whoever refuses this becomes unhinged and his purpose miscarries.

But this acceptance is only a first stage. To over-adapt oneself is to give oneself up to the bondage of things. The aim of comfort turns man into the domestic animal of the things that provide his comfort; it degrades his productive or social function to automatism. Man's exploitation of nature is not destined to erect upon the web of natural determinism another net-work of conditional reflexes; it is to open up, before the creative liberty of an ever-increasing number of men, the highest possibilities of human being. It is the force of personal affirmation which breaks down the obstacles and opens the way: and to this end we have to deny nature as it is given while affirming it as a task—a task which is both personal and the condition of all personality. Only then, when the *belonging* to nature turns into the *mastery* of nature, is the world joined to the body and man to his proper destiny.

But we must give its correct meaning to this action of man on nature.

Such action cannot, without disaster, give itself up to the frenzy of its own acceleration—to what Henry Ford was admitting in his reply to the question why he went on for ever developing his enterprise,—"Because I can't stop myself!"

It does not consist in subjecting things to the relationship of a slave under a master. The person achieves freedom only in conferring it: and is called to liberate things as well as humanity. Marx used to say of capitalism that its reduction of things to commodities degrades them: to be made merely instrumental to profit deprives the things themselves of the intrinsic dignity which poets, for example, see in them. We contribute to this degradation whenever we use things as mere obstacles to be overcome, as stuff to be possessed or dominated. The arbitrary power we then presume to exercise over things soon communicates itself to human relations, infusing them

12

with tyranny; for tyranny originates always in man, never from things. The Marxist movement, with its belief that the mission of mankind is, on the contrary, to elevate the status of things through the humanization of nature, in this respect approaches the Christian doctrine that the destiny of man is to redeem, both by labour and through his own redemption, the nature that has been corrupted with his fall. The supreme value that is claimed, by Marxism, for man's practical activity (*praxis*), is a kind of secularization of the central value that the Christian tradition claims for work.[1]

The relation of the person with nature is not, then, a purely exterior one, but is a dialectic of exchange, and of ascension. Man presses down upon nature to overcome nature, as the aeroplane rests its weight on the air in order to free itself from weight. Ever since man's first appearance upon the earth— 'to cultivate and to tend it' (Genesis II.15.) and to give names to all creatures—there has been no absolute nature, but only nature in process of humanization. So-called nature is interspersed throughout with man's artifices. Yet we have hardly been able, since our history began, to do more than begin clumsily to learn how to understand and administer the world. We are now but beginning to enter into its secrets, those of matter, of life and of the psyche. This is a critical turning-point. As the *Essays of Feuerbach* announce in a tone of triumph, henceforth we are going to *transform* as much as to *explain*. Wisdom is to take up industry. Industry will make mistakes: but will it make more of them than philosophy has done? In this sense, *to produce* is indeed an essential activity of the person, for production is viewed in a perspective so sublime that the more menial activities are caught up in the wind of the spirit that lifts humanity above itself. Shackled at first to the immediate satisfaction of elementary needs, then loosened from them by parasitic interests or betrayed to its own infatuations, production should at last become an activity both liberated and liberating, shaped

[1] *Esprit*, special number: *Le travail et l'homme*, July 1933

by *all* the requirements of personality. Upon that condition, the mandate of economics, wherever it rightly rules, is the mandate of mankind. But production has value only in regard to its highest end, which is the advent of the world of persons. It cannot derive value from the organization of techniques, nor from the accumulation of products, nor purely and simply as the means to prosperity.

By this light alone can we grasp the profound meaning of technical development. Man is unique in his invention of tools, and in his subsequent linking of them into systems of machinery that slowly frame a collective body for all humanity. The men of this twentieth century are bewildered to see this new and all powerful body they are constructing. The power of abstraction in the machine is indeed frightening: by its severance of human contacts, it can make us forget, more dangerously than anything else has ever done, what happens to those whose work it controls and whose bodies it may sacrifice. Perfectly objective, altogether explicable, it de-educates us from all that is intimate, secret or inexpressible. It puts undreamed-of powers into the hands of imbeciles: it entertains us by its excesses, only to distract us from its cruelties. Left to its own blind inertia, it is the most powerful of forces making for depersonalization. It is all these things, however, only when regarded apart from the spirit that is promoting it as a means to the liberation of man from natural servitude, and to the reconquest of nature. Any purely negative attitude towards technical development springs from inadequate analysis, or from some idealist notion of a destiny that we can only imagine as a subjection to the forces of the earth. The technical age will indeed menace man's progress towards personalization with the greatest possible dangers, just as the rapid growth of an adolescent's body threatens to upset his equilibrium. But this is a development immune to our maledictions. And far from being a disastrous error of European particularism, it may yet prove to be the means by which man will one day invade the universe, extending his kingdom until his imagination is at last set free from the fear that his conscious mind, for all its glory, is only a paradox adrift in the infinite inane.

Checks upon the personalization of nature
The tragic optimism

When we trace, with a kind of triumphant amplitude, the vistas of destiny that are opened up by the urge of personalization, let us never forget that its future is by no means automatically assured. At every moment, some new difficulty refers this prospect back to the personal decision of each of us, and it is prejudiced by each and all of our derelictions. For matter is rebellious, not only passive, it is aggressive and not merely inert. Personalism, to borrow a phrase from Maurice Nédoncelle, is not 'a philosophy for Sunday afternoons'. Wherever the person directs its illumination, nature, the body or matter inserts its opacity, beclouding the formula of the scientist, the clarity of reason, or even the transparency of love. Whenever liberty spreads its wings, nature finds numerous ways to depress its flight. When we move towards intimate knowledge, nature externalizes, extends and generalizes. A gain in sensitivity can be a loss of sensation; species spring from a recession of life; habit and custom harden with the lack of invention and laws from the decline of love.[1] Beset by the personal universe, nature ceaselessly threatens to besiege it in her turn. There is nothing in the relation between personal man and the world that suggests the 'pre-established harmony' of Leibnitz. Insecurity and trouble are our lot. Nor does anything suggest that the struggle will end in some predictable time or manner;[2]

---

[1] For this theme of objectivisation, see above all BERDYAEV, especially his *Esprit et Liberté* (Je sers); *La Destination de l'homme* (Je sers); *Cinq Meditations sur l'existence* (Aubier).

[2] Etienne *De Greef* in his important works *Notre Destinée et nos instincts* (Plon); *Les Instincts de défense et de sympathie* (Presses Universitaires) treats this subject in a rather pessimistic way.

we have no reason to doubt that it is constitutive of our condition. The perfection of the embodied personal universe, therefore, is not the perfection of an order, as it is in all the philosophic (and all the political) systems which pretend that man will one day totalise the world. It is the perfection of a liberty that is militant, locked in combat, subsisting indeed by the limits it overcomes. Between the impatient optimism of liberal and revolutionary illusion, and the impatient pessimism of the fascists, the right road for man is in this tragic optimism, where he finds his true destiny in a goal of greatness through unending struggle.

CHAPTER II

COMMUNICATION

HITHERTO we have been describing the person in universal terms. We must now try to see what it is in fundamental experience. Common opinion notwithstanding, the fundamental nature of the person is not originality nor self-knowledge nor individual affirmation. It lies not in separation but in communication.

THE SELF-DEFENCE OF THE INDIVIDUAL

Personalism opposed to individualism

For a spectator of the human drama who is not blind to his own reactions, this truth is far from self-evident. From the beginnings of history until now, there have been many more days spent in war than in peace. The life of societies is a perpetual guerrilla, and where hostility dies down, indifference supervenes. All the efforts of comradeship, of friendship and love seem futile against the vast obstacles to human brotherhood. Heidegger and Sartre make much of this in their philosophy. For them, the need to possess and to overcome everlastingly obstructs communication. Associated man is necessarily either tyrant or slave. The very look of another steals somewhat of my universe, his presence restricts my liberty, his promotion is my demotion. As for love, it is a mutual disease, an inferno.

It is in vain to protest against this view. It is also hard to deny the importance of the aspect of human relations that it presents. The world of others is no garden of delight: it is a perpetual provocation to self-diminishment or aggrandisement. It continually re-imposes risk and suffering just as we seem to be achieving peace. Even the refusal to recognize this springs from the instinct of self-defence. Some, trying to forget it, narrow all their social contacts. Others make themselves into the pliable and useful objects of those around them—they become the poor of the philanthropists, the juniors of this man or the servants of that; while the egoists take flight from all altruism as illusion. Yet another may restrict his circle to people who consent to act as his own mirror. A kind of instinct works continually within us to deny or diminish the humanity of those around us. [1]

Even if his disposition is of the best, the individual darkens communication by his very presence, which produces some degree of opacity whoever he is. My body itself gives me the most obvious image of this opacity, interposing its hindrance in the midst of every confidence. But it arises from something deeper than the body. A virtue over-emphasized arouses distaste for virtue, the will to seduce disillusions love, and the will to convert the infidel puts up his hackles. The lightest touch of the individual seems sometimes to inject a mortal poison into any contact between man and man.

Over these depths of separatism, culture stages its play of masks, painted and re-painted until the mask and the face of the individual are hardly distinguishable. The masks are only the means to a double purpose, which is to deceive oneself as well as others, and to find in mutual imposture a refuge from the truth which flashes out whenever one sees another from without precisely as he sees himself within.

Individualism is a system of morals, feelings, ideas and institutions in which individuals can be organized by their mutual isolation and defence. This was the ideology and the

[1] Cf. E. MOUNIER: *Traité du caractère,* Chap. IX. *Introduction aux existentialismes,* Chap. V.

prevailing structure of Western bourgeois society in the 18th and 19th centuries. Man in the abstract, unattached to any natural community, the sovereign lord of a liberty unlimited and undirected; turning towards others with a primary mistrust, calculation and self-vindication; institutions restricted to the assurance that these egoisms should not encroach upon one another, or to their betterment as a purely profitmaking association—such is the rule of civilization now breaking up before our eyes, one of the poorest history has known. It is the very antithesis of personalism, and its dearest enemy.

For this reason 'the person' is sometimes opposed to 'the individual'. In this, however, there is some risk of dividing the person from his concrete attachments. The self-reflective movement which constitutes 'the individual' contributes to the maintenance of the human shape. But the person is only growing in so far as he is continually purifying himself from the individual within him. He cannot do this by force of self-attention, but on the contrary by making himself *available* (Gabriel Marcel) and thereby more transparent both to himself and to others. Things then happen as though the person, no longer 'occupied with himself' or 'full of himself', were becoming able—then and thus only—to be someone else and to enter into grace.

Communication as primordial fact

Thus, if the first condition of individualism is the centralization of the individual in himself, the first condition of personalism is his decentralization, in order to set him in the open perspectives of personal life.

The latter begins at a very early age. The first movement that reveals the human being in infancy is its recognition of others: the baby of six to twelve months emerging from its vegetative state, discovers itself in those around it, learns about itself through its responses to those who look after it. Only later, about the third year, do we see the first signs of egocentric reflection. We are easily misled, when we think about the person, by its external image; we place ourselves over against it as if it were an object. But my body is also, to myself, a vacancy, an eye wide-open to the world in self-forgetfulness. In its inner experience[1] the person is a presence directed towards the world and other persons, mingled among them in universal space. Other persons do not limit it, they enable it to be and to grow. The person only exists thus towards others, it only knows itself in knowing others, only finds itself in being known by them. The *thou*, which implies the *we*, is prior to the *I*—or at least accompanies it. It is in material nature (to which we are only partly subject) that we find mutual limitation and exclusion, because a space cannot contain two things at once. But the person, by the movement which is its being, *ex-poses* itself. It is thus communicable by its nature, and it is lonely from the need to communicate. We must start from that primordial fact. Just as a philosopher who from the start confines himself to thinking never finds the doorway to being, the man who begins by shutting himself in himself never finds the way towards others. When communication fails or is corrupted, I suffer an essential loss of myself: every kind of madness is a severance of my relations with others—*alter* then becomes *alienus*, and I in my turn become a stranger to myself, alienated. One might almost say that I have no existence, save in so far as I exist for others, and that to be is, in the final analysis, to love.

These truths are so essential to personalism that it would be a pleonasm to point out that the civilization it seeks is both "personalist and communal".[2] In opposition to individualism

---

[1] Cf. Maurice NEDONCELLE *La réciprocité des consciences* (Aubier);
BUBER *Je et tu* (Aubier)
MADINIER *Conscience et amour* (Presses Universitaires)
The Germans say: my being is *being-with*, *Mitsein*, or is *being towards*, *Zusein*. Cf. also the Latin; *adsum* 'here I am' (*to* you, at your disposal).

[2] This is the formula used in *Esprit* in special numbers published in the winter of '32—'33: *Révolution personnaliste*, *Révolution communautaire*, and in E. MOUNIER: *Révolution personnaliste et communautaire* (Aubier 1934) many times reprinted since then.

and to whatever idealism still persists, personalism demonstrates that the human subject cannot be nourished by auto-digestion; that one can possess only so much as one gives, or only that to which one gives oneself; and that no one can find salvation, either spiritual or social, in himself.

The primary action of the person, therefore, is to sustain, together with others, a society of persons, the structure, the customs, the sentiments and the institutions of which are shaped by their nature as persons; a society whose moral constitution we are as yet only beginning faintly to discern.

This development is founded upon a series of original actions, to which there is no equivalent elsewhere in the whole universe:

(1) *Going out of the self.* The person being capable of detachment from itself, of self-dispossession, of decentralizing itself in order to become available for others. In the personalist tradition (in Christianity especially) the ascetic of self-dispossession is the central ascetic of the personal life. Only those who are thus liberated can ever liberate others or the world. The ancients used to talk of the overcoming of self-love: nowadays we call self-love ego-centricity, narcissism, or individualism.

(2) *Understanding.* This is ceasing to see myself from my own point of view, and looking at myself from the standpoint of others. Not looking for myself in someone else chosen for his likeness to me, nor seeking to know another according to some general knowledge (a taste for psychology is not an interest in other persons) but accepting his singularity with my own, in an action that welcomes him, and in an effort that re-centres myself. It is to be all things to all men, but without ceasing to be, or to be myself. For there is a manner of understanding everyone which is equivalent to loving nothing and ceasing to be anything—a merging of oneself with others that is not a comprehension of them.[1]

(3) *Taking upon oneself—sharing—*the destiny, the troubles,

[1] Cf. J. LACROIX : *Le sens du rèalism* (Ed. Lea Baconnière)

the joy or the task of another; taking him 'upon one's heart'.

(4) *Giving.* The vitality of the personal impulse is to be found neither in self-defence (as in petty-bourgeois individualism) nor in life-and-death struggle (as with existentialism) but in *generosity* or *self-bestowal*—ultimately, in giving without measure and without hope of reward. The economic of personality is an economic of donation, not of compensation nor of calculation. Generosity dissolves the opacity and annuls the solitude of the subject, even when it calls forth no response: but its impact upon the serried ranks of opposing instincts, interests and reasonings can be truly irresistible. It disarms refusal by offering to another what is of eminent value in his own estimation, at the very moment when he might expect to be over-ridden as an obstacle, and he is himself caught in its contagion: hence the great liberating value of forgiveness, and of confidence. Generosity fails only in the face of certain resentments more mysterious than those of contrary interest, hatreds which seem to be directed against disinterestedness itself.

(5) *Faithfulness.* The adventure of the person is one that is continuous from birth to death. Devotion to the person, therefore, love or friendship, cannot be perfect except in continuity. This continuity is not a mere prolongation or repetition of the same thing, like that of a material or logical generalization: it is a perpetual renewal. Personal faithfulness is creative faithfulness.[1]

This dialectic of personal intercourse builds up and sustains the being of all who participate in it.

Whenever I treat another person as though he were not present, or as a repository of information for my use (G. Marcel), an instrument at my disposal; or when I set him down in a list without right of appeal—in such a case I am behaving towards him as though he were an object, which means in effect,

[1] Upon this theme of fidelity, see G. MARCEL: *Etre et Avoir, Du Refus à l'invocation.*

despairing of him. But if I treat him as a subject, as a presence—which is to recognize that I am unable to define or classify him, that he is inexhaustible, filled with hopes upon which alone he can act—this is to give him credit. To despair of anyone is to make him desperate: whereas the credit that generosity extends regenerates his own confidence. It acts as the appeal (Jaspers' 'invocation') that nourishes the spirit. They are mistaken who speak of love as self-identification. That is only true of sympathy,[1] or of those 'elective affinities' in which one is seeking to assimilate more of some good quality, or to find some resonance of oneself in someone similar. Real love is creative of distinction; it is a gratitude and a will towards another because he is other than oneself. Sympathy is after all an affinity of nature, while love is a new state of being. It speaks to the subject from beyond his nature; it wills his realization as a person, in perfect liberty, whatever his gifts or disadvantages may be; for these are without essential importance in love. Love may be blind; but it has 'second sight'.

This communion of love, in liberating him who responds to it, also liberates and reassures him who offers it. Love is the surest certainty that man knows; the one irrefutable, existential *cogito:* I love, therefore I am; therefore being is, and life has value (is worth the pain of living). Love does not reassure me simply as a state of being in which I find myself, for it gives me to someone else. Sartre has spoken of the eye of another as something that transfixes one, that curdles the blood; and of the presence of someone else as a trespass upon one, a deprivation or a bondage. What we speak of here is no less disturbing; it shakes me out of my self-assurance, my habits, my egocentric torpor: communication, even when hostile, is the thing that most surely reveals me to myself.

[1] Which SCHELER sharply distinguishes from love: *On the Nature and Forms of Sympathy.* (Trans. In preparation, Routledge & Kegan Paul). Cf. also MADINIER op. cit., LE SENNE *Introduction à la psychologie*, Chap. IX, concerning the different meanings of the word 'we'.

Thus the positive interpersonal relation is a reciprocal provocation, a mutual fertilization.

Obstacles to communication

But personal being is not loving from morning till night. Communication is hindered by various obstacles.

(1) Something of the other person invariably eludes our most whole-hearted efforts to communicate. In the most intimate of conversations, perfect accord is not vouchsafed to us. We can never be certain that there may not be some admixture of misunderstanding, except in those rare, miraculous moments when the certitude of what is communicated is too strong for any analysis—and one such moment can be the passport to a whole life. But such is the profound loneliness of love; from which, the more perfect love is, the more it suffers.

(2) There is something in us that deeply opposes every movement toward reciprocity, the kind of fundamental ill-will that we have already mentioned.

(3) There is an irreducible opacity about our very manner of existing, giving rise to a curiosity that ceaselessly raises up barriers between our minds.

(4) Any relationship of reciprocity that we may form—that of the family, of the nation, of the religious community, etc.— soon engenders a new egocentricity of its own, erecting yet another screen between man and man.

Thus, in reality, and in the universe in which we actually live, the person is far more often exposed to others than protected by them, is more isolated than incorporated. Personality is an eagerness for friendship, even where the whole world of persons is closed to it; and yet communion is rarer than happiness, more fragile than beauty. A trifle can check or break it, even between two subjects; how then can we hope for it between a greater number? "The universe of conscious subjects makes one think of a machine with its driving-belts all broken, its wheels revolving in disorder" (Nédoncelle); or, as G. Marcel has it, a broken world.

One may ascribe this to institutions which perpetuate the struggle of classes and the oppression of man by man. But who can say whether these institutions are really the cause or the effect? One has to fight against them, for neither here nor elsewhere is it enough to appeal to fine sentiments; the structures of our social life are parasitic upon personality; and it is only by supplanting them with other structures that we can eliminate what remains of individualism. But it is no less necessary to understand and maintain the purpose of such a development. The solitude that so many writers of today present as a given condition of human life is for the most part of our own contrivance; we isolate ourselves.

Community or Collectivity

After these reflections, one may be surprised to find that personalism is sometimes represented as a reaction against collectivism. In its name the communal is sometimes opposed to the collective; we are expected to sigh over the lost little communities—the village, the workshop and the family—and to disseminate fear of the greater associations. There are grave misunderstandings in this attitude. It implies an abuse of the mystique of *nearness* as well as of *smallness*. Whenever man has had to confront an enlargement of his sphere of action, he has been seized by the same panic, the same feeling of being menaced or rendered derelict. Each time he has invoked, as he is doing today, associations 'worthy of human dignity' or within 'the measure of man'. But within what measure is man himself made? Is he made to the scale of the suburban garden and rural neighbourhood, or to that of the universe and history? A being who thinks in terms of millions of miles above his head and of millionths of millimetres in work under his hands, a being who is expected to read and to make universal history, is not measured by the length of his stride. It can indeed be mischievous to mix human beings together in great masses; undoubtedly we need to study the effects of such action in the living experience of smaller associations. Here, the criticism of social gigantism arouses a salutary disquietude in opposition to those who, infatuated with logic or with power, think of men by masses, the better to think of them as instruments or as so much matter, and the better to disregard them as persons. But if this critique requires us to articulate social relations and to observe the criteria of scale and of the optimum in matters of human grouping, it does not command us, in any way, to impose once for all a standard model for human societies. The scale of an association differs according to the human relationship concerned: by all the evidence, it is not the same—to take the two extremes—in friendship as in a modern economic society.

The truth is that this anti-collectivism conceals an underlying nostalgia for a puristic notion of a society of persons which is impossible. In practical fact, communication is generally delegated; it is entrusted, by the mystical community in which all liberties are interfused, to the social order in which activities are co-ordinated and structurally related. Obviously, social structure impoverishes personal relations, because it is only able to ensure continuity by means of repetition. An angelic family would, presumably, abound without ceasing in deeds of mutual love; an angelic economy in the circulation of gifts. But a real family is also a psychological and juridical constraint, and a human economy is a network of rules and obligations. There is an inherent danger in this partly impersonal character of social structure; but it is not only a danger. In relation to the desire for communion it is what the body is to the personal aspiration, both a resistance and a necessary foothold. To reject this because of its ambivalence is to seek to escape from the human condition: the dreams of the anarchists, moving though some of them may be, either end in impotence or oscillate between utter catastrophism and an ingenuous conformism.

Personalism, therefore, refuses to attach a pejorative co-efficient to social existence or to its collective structures: it seeks to delineate, however, a hierarchy of collectivities, according to the degree of their communal potential, that is, according to whether they are more, or less, personal in structure or in operation.

At the lowest level on which a human universe can subsist, we find what Heidegger calls One's world,[1] the state in which one allows oneself to be simply aggregated with the others, ceasing to be a lucid and responsible subject. This is the world of consciousness half asleep, of obscure instincts, of vague opinion, human respect and worldly relations, of daily gossip, of social and political pliability, of moral mediocrity, of the crowd, the anonymous mass, of the irresponsible apparatus of life. It is a devitalized, desolate world in which every person provisionally renounces himself quâ person, to become some-thing, it matters not what, that is interchangeable. 'One's world' constitutes neither a *we* nor a *whole*. It is not bound up with this or that form of society, but is a manner of existing in any of them. The first act of personal life is an awakening to the consciousness of this anonymous life and a revolt against the degradation that it represents.

At a rather higher level, vital societies, of a more indivi-dualised 'consciousness', remain nevertheless bound to their functions, and though function co-ordinates it does not deeply unite. A family which knows no ties but those of the blood can easily become a nest of vipers. A community limited to needs and interests bears the seeds of discord within its pro-visional concord, for, contrary to the beliefs of the liberal moralists, merely customary co-operation never leads self-interest out of its egocentric grooves. Moreover, vital societies, insufficiently personalized, are gregarious, tend towards self-hypnosis, arrogance and war; the internal hierarchy of functions,

---

[1] The point of the phrase is the impersonal pronoun: as in saying 'at Rome, *one* does as the Romans do' (*Trans.*)

if it reigns supreme, hardens into a relation of masters and slaves, of classes, castes etc., giving occasion for internal wars. Such societies tend to form a *whole* which corrupts the *we*. They do not remain hospitable to the person, unless they are subordinate to some superior order.

In the 18th century it was believed that the one way of escape from the passions of irrational societies would be a reasonable society, based upon the reconciliation of men's minds in an impersonal philosophy and the harmonising of their behaviour within a system of formal, juridical rights. Given compulsory education, industrial organization and the rule of law, men thought they would be well on the way to universal peace. Experience should have warned them that knowledge does not convert men's hearts, that formal rights may be abused to conceal rebellious wrongs; that organization and ideology, if pursued in disregard of the personal absolute, can be corrupted by passion into police-rule, cruelty and war —in short, that no universal harmony can be established at the expense of the person. It is an outraged consciousness of having been deceived by these illusions, and an emotional desolation at the loss of them, which have driven the masses, during recent years, into a frenzy of irrational *mystiques*— fascism, absurdism, psychoanalysis, esotericism, and so forth.

We shall certainly not repair this disintegration, this collective neurosis, by a return to rationalistic illusions. Nor, equally certainly, by trying to discredit the mediating power of reason. Thought can only exist and radiate its illumination in the incarnate subject. If thought does not make itself communicable, and therefore in a sense impersonal, it is not thought but delirium. Science and objective reason are the indispensable conditions of inter-subjectivity. And legal right also is no less necessary as a mediator: it curbs biological egoism; it guarantees each person's existence; it ensures, in the jungle of instincts and urges, a minimum of security in which the seeds of personal life can germinate.[1] It is necessary to bear in mind, at one and the same time, the absolute necessity of these mediations, and their inability to ensure the fullness of personal community.

Perfect community, at least at the present stage of our experience, can hardly be attained even between two, or among a very few, persons; lovers, friends, a little group of comrades, believers in the same religion or fighters in the same cause. Even so, the communal spirit is liable swiftly to evaporate, so that the best of these associations is in danger of lapsing into a closed society. They can only continue as elements of a personal universe in so far as each keeps itself open in spirit to all the others.

Concerning the unity of persons

The nature of the person now discloses its fundamental tension. It is constituted by a double movement, contradictory in appearance but in fact dialectical, on the one hand towards the affirmation of personal absolutes that resist any limitation, and on the other towards the creation of a universal union of the world of persons.

This union cannot be one of identical beings: the person is, by definition, that which cannot be duplicated or repeated.

Nevertheless, there is a world of persons. If they formed an absolute plurality it would be impossible for one among them, you or I, to think them all at once, to apply the common name of person to them. There must be some common factor. Contemporary thought is repudiating the idea of an abiding human nature, since it is becoming aware of still unexplored possibilities in our condition. It rejects the conception of 'human nature' as a prejudice that would limit these possibilities in

---

[1] Cf. GURVITCH: *L'idée du droit social* (Sirey); Jean LACROIX: *Personne et amour* (Edition du Livre Français); RENOUVIER's remarks upon the transition from the state of war to that of peace, and the *Opuscules sur l'histoire* of KANT.

advance. And indeed, they are often so astonishing that we ought not to ascribe limits to them without the greatest reserve. But it is one thing to reject the tyranny of formal definitions and quite another to deny, as existentialism sometimes does, that man has any one essence or constitution. If every man *is* nothing but what he *makes himself*, there can be no humanity, no history and no community (which indeed is the conclusion that certain existentialists end by accepting).

Personalism therefore includes among its leading ideas, the affirmation of the *unity of mankind*, both in space and time, which was foreshadowed by certain schools of thought in the latter days of antiquity and confirmed in the Judeo-Christian tradition. For the Christian there are neither citizens nor barbarians, neither bond nor free, neither Jew nor gentile, neither white, black or yellow, but only men created in the image of God and called to salvation in Christ. The conception of a human race with a collective history and destiny, from which no individual destiny can be separated, is one of the sovereign ideas of the Fathers of the Church. In a secularised form, this is the animating principle of eighteenth century cosmopolitanism, and later of Marxism. It is flatly opposed to the ideas of absolute discontinuity between free spirits (as in Sartre) or between civilizations (in Malraux or Frobenius). It is against every form of racialism or of caste, against the 'elimination of the abnormal', the contempt of the foreigner, against the totalitarians' denigration of political adversaries —in short, it is altogether against the fabrication of scape-goats. Any man, however different, or even degraded, remains a man, for whom we ought to make a human way of life possible.

This sense of humanity as one and indivisible, is strictly implicit in the modern notion of *equality*. The formulas in which this equality is sometimes expressed are misleading upon this point: far from being an individualistic and dis-sociative conception, the idea of relatedness is essential to it. It has been invoked in condemnation of old, sclerotic communities, only in order that men might rediscover the living principle of community at a profounder level. Similarly, the contemporary idea of *justice* wears, on the face of it, an aspect of individual self-defence, because justice has continually to be reclaimed from nature, which is perpetually producing new inequalities. Yet justice is both a rule and an obedience (Proudhon). These ideas cut far deeper, then, than traditionalist criticism will admit. "Equality," writes G. Madinier, "is what the external life of individuals becomes, when they aspire to the attainment of a moral community." This felicitous formula exemplifies both the richness and the limitations of such notions. They over-estimate the power of formal reason and positive law, misunderstanding on the one hand the force of instinct and on the other the spontaneity of love. Renouvier and Proudhon tended to place love beyond reason but upon the level of natural vitality, not above it. Thus they inclined to emphasize the plurality of individuals in their distrust of the passional or political mystifications which we have to cope with today, if we are to liberate men from their parasitic fears. But we must aim higher than this: as someone has said— justice looks higher than it can reach.

Whither—towards the final end of mankind? Yes, provided always that we detach the idea of this final aim from biological associations; just as we had to separate the idea of equality from arithmetical implications. In the living world, the final end or cause implies strict subordination of the parts to the whole and of the parts themselves to the pattern of their complementary functions. Such a structure is inappropriate to a society of spiritual subjects, each of whom has its end in itself and in the whole at the same time: it would subject them to an organization of a totalitarian character, such as we find in certain primitive societies that are 'communist' in an older sense of the word. In our days, this would amount to pure technocracy. But the viability of an organization depends upon its members, and its sphere of development is the universe of persons. Otherwise this development, instead of liberating man, brings about a new state of nature, a conflict of 'masses', a régime of industrial armies and their leaders, in which persons are less than pawns. 'Totalitarianism' is well named: the world of persons is that which can never be added up to a total.

So much for the movement towards unification in the personal universe: we must now go on to distinguish, in that universe, the elements of internal differentiation and tension.

CHAPTER III

THE INTIMATE CONVERSION

IF the person is, from the beginning, a movement towards others (being-towards) from another point of view it reveals something else, no less distinctive, the pulsation of a secret life which is the ceaseless spring of its productivity. We would apply to this the customary names of *subjectivity* or *inner life* or *inwardness*, but that these words call up an ambiguous spatial image, and would seem to centre the personal life in a movement of withdrawal, whereas, as we shall see, it is not the opposite of communication we are here concerned with, but its complement.

Self-recollection (*the higher self*)

Here is a stone on my desk. It has existence, but it exists somewhat as a crossroads, it is what it is made to be by an interplay of forces that it represents, and it is nothing more. The animal world is the beginning of a break with existence thus devoid of interior dimension; it fashions the external world into a fitting environment for its own biological performance. Man is capable of living like a thing; but since he is not a thing, he feels that to live like one is a dereliction of duty: it is the 'distraction' of Pascal, the 'aesthetic stage' of Kierkegaard, the 'inauthentic life' of Heidegger, the 'alienation' of Marx, the 'self-deception'[1] of Sartre. Man thus distracting himself is living as though exiled from himself, immersed in the tumult of the outer world: such a man is the

[1] "*Mauvaise foi.*" See SARTRE; Existentialism and Humanism (Methuen)

33

prisoner of his appetites, his functions, his habits, his relations; of the world in which he merely diverts himself. This is the 'immediate' life, without memory, without plan, without mastery; such is the very definition of externality, or, more simply, of vulgarity. Personal life begins with the ability to break contact with the environment, to recollect oneself, to reflect, in order to re-constitute and re-unite oneself on one's own centre.

At first sight this is a movement of withdrawal. But the withdrawal is only a moment in a more complex movement. If, as in certain cases, the withdrawal is a psychic contortion in which the subject becomes fixed, some abnormality has come into play. Normally, what is important is not the act of withdrawal but the accompanying concentration. The person has only drawn backward the better to go forward.

From this essential experience follow the values of silence and of retreat, never more widely forgotten nor more needful of remembrance than they are today. The distractions of our civilization are eating away the sense of leisure, the respect for the flight of time, the patience that waits for good work to come to maturity: they are drowning that voice of the silence which, it is to be feared, no one except the poet and the man of religion will much longer be able to hear.

The very vocabulary of contemplation (*e.g.* self-recollection, concentration) reminds us, however, that this is an act of conquest, the opposite of a naïve confidence in spontaneity or internal fantasy. Our chief enemy, says G. Marcel, is that which appears to us to be 'quite natural', that which *goes on by itself* according to instinct or habit: for we cannot naïvely become persons. Nevertheless the action of meditation is also one of simplification: it is not a psychological complication or refinement. It seeks what is central; and it goes straight thither. This has nothing to do with rumination or morbid introspection. It begins as an act, and it issues in action.

The secret (the inmost self)

What is this contemplation searching the depths in order to find? A formula? Personal meditation undoubtedly avails itself of concepts, diagrams and systems.[1] One must not go too fast in calling up the ineffable. But to explain is, by definition, to let go of the singular, of that which is one and indivisible. The person is not 'something' that one can find at the end of an analysis, nor is it a definable combination of characteristics. If it were a sum-total, the items could be listed: but this is the reality whose contents *cannot be put into an inventory* (G. Marcel). If they could, it would be determined by them; but the person is self-determining and free. It is a *presence* rather than a being, a presence that is active, without limits. Contemporary psychology has explored several infernal regions in its depths; but has paid less attention to what one might call the heavenly abysses into which its creative exaltation and mystical life ascend. Neither psychology nor the intimations of art have succeeded more than slightly in portraying either these depths or these heights.

We know that the personal life is related by its nature to something *secret*. Some people are wholly extraverted, thoroughly exhibited; they have no secret, no contents, no background. They are like open books, and quickly read. Having no experience of any depth, they have no 'respect for privacy', their own or anyone else's. They have an unrefined taste for talking and for making others talk, for gossip and curious enquiry. Now, discretion and reserve are the homage that the person renders to the sense of an infinite life within. Since this infinitude can never be fully expressed by direct communication, the person sometimes prefers indirect communication —irony, humour, paradox, myth, symbol, pretence etc.

In writings of a personalist inspiration,[2] one frequently finds discussions on the theme of *modesty*. Modesty arises

[1] Cf. E. MOUNIER : *Traité du caractère*. Chp. I.
[2] For examples—Kierkegaard, Jaspers, Solovyov.

from the fact that the person feels itself to be something more than any expression of itself, and menaced in its very being when anyone takes its manifest existence for its total existence. Physical modesty signifies, not that the body is impure, but that I am immeasurably more than a body that can be seen or touched. Modesty about my feelings, is the recognition that all of them limit and some can betray me. Both kinds of modesty mean that I am not to be made the sport of nature, nor of other persons. I am not ashamed of this nakedness, nor of that personal trait, but of seeming to be nothing more than they. The opposite of modesty is vulgarity, allowing myself to be merely what I am in immediate appearance, in the glare of the public eye.

Presently, however, we shall have to deal faithfully with false modesties and with the morbid feeling of secrecy.

Intimacy. Privacy

In the warm shelter of certain personal experiences, we find a kind of plenitude of life—the feeling of intimacy, which is not a simple feeling. It represents the joy of a return to the internal sources of being for refreshment. But this experience is often adulterated by a vegetative relish for what is snug and shut-in, for feelings like those of the embryo within the mother or of the infant in her arms, magically isolated and protected from all other contacts. This feeling of being *at home*, which is a fusion of various elements, is profoundly ambivalent. It may mark a moment when I am giving up the fight for personality; in which case it represents a dereliction, even though it assume all the values commonly attached to a contemplative withdrawal. And it is around this focus of ambiguities that the sphere of *private life* is established. Between my secret life and my public life, here is the field where I seek to maintain my social being in profound peace, in the intimate discourse of persons with persons. But it is also the place where I may be seeking a tepid life, a vegetative passivity, or a biological dependence. The praises of the reflective life, of a retired life, of the family etc., too often betray this dubious origin.

However, man must on no account play at being pure spirit. Compounded of light and earth as we are, we could not attain the sanctuaries of the person without passing some portion of our life in vegetative peace; but we need to watch for the moment when this threatens to slow down the vivacity of the spirit; when what used to be frank and welcoming in personal intimacies begins to be unresponsive and exclusive. It is at this point that modesty hardens into prudery, while reserve degenerates into secretiveness, distant behaviour or mannerism. The bourgeois conduct of private life has been conspicuously liable to such corruption, with its multiplication of pseudo-secrets (secrets of business, of the household, of illness, domestic disorders, etc.).

Totalitarian governments adduce this over-sophistication in justification of their attempts to do away with private life altogether. It is to be suspected, however, that they attempt this more in fear of the profound resources of private life than in dislike of its perversions. All that is really needed is to demystify private life; to prevent its being a privileged rampart against the public welfare. The very structure of personal life itself requires no less: for *reflection* is not simply a turning of the power of consciousness back upon the self and its imaginations; it is also *intention*, a *projection* of the self. There is not, e.g., a tree over there, and an image of that tree enclosed within me as if in a box, beheld by an eye of consciousness somewhere behind the lid. To be conscious of the tree is to be over there, amongst its leaves and branches: it is even in some sense, as the Hindus and certain romantics have said, *to be* that tree, palpitating with it in the sweet fever of spring, feeling its century-old boughs in my own limbs, breaking out into joy with its budding—and yet to remain myself, distinct from it. Intimate consciousness is no back dressing-room in which the person cons his own part. It is like the light itself, a presence inscrutable in itself, which yet reveals and illuminates the entire visible universe.

The vertigo of the Abyss

The familiar enjoyments of intimacy are but one aspect of the personal life. To withdraw from agitation is not always to find repose. A man who retires within himself but, instead of stopping in the calm of the first resting-place, resolves to continue his adventure to the ultimate end of self-knowledge, soon finds himself far from any help. Certain artists, mystics, and philosophers have pursued, to the point of self-destruction, their experiences of this 'inner life'—rather oddly so-called, for it may send one fleeing to the four corners of the world. One hears much, in these days, of 'anguish'—far too much. What is commonly meant by this is no more than the psychological sympton of an epoch of social aimlessness, a product of disintegration. But beside this pathological anguish, there is indeed an essential anguish, arising within personal existence as such, from the terrifying mystery of its liberty, from the realization of its mortal struggle, and from the wild explorations to which it is impelled in every direction. This vertigo of the great depths is such that all the means employed to allay it —indifference, conciliation, comfort, false reassurance or harsh repression—end in the futility of swindle or make-believe: but they would amount to slow spiritual suicide or the sterilization of existence, if they did not crumble to nothing at the first serious challenge of reality.

From appropriation to disappropriation

Personal life is an alternation of self-affirmation and self-denial. This fundamental rhythm can be discerned in all its manifestations. The self-affirmation is a continual assimilation of external data, in working upon which it enriches itself. As we have seen, pure subjectivity is humanly unthinkable.

To have at its own disposal a certain range of objects, with which it can form relations of intimacy somewhat like those that it seeks with other persons, relations of frequency and of long duration—this is, for the person, an elementary need. Self-affirmation is first of all to give oneself scope and living-space. It is, therefore, a mistake to set up too sharp an opposition between 'being' and 'having'[1] as if these were mutually exclusive alternatives and we had to make an existential choice between them. We should think of them rather as polar opposites between which our embodied existence is held in tension. It is just not possible to be without having, true though it is that personal being is an indefinite capacity of having, that it is never fulfilled in whatsoever it may have, and that its meaning transcends all having. Yet without having it would have no *hold* on the object but would fade away into it. To possess is, moreover, to make contact, to give up one's isolation, to 'bear with' something. It is possible for 'poverty' to be spurious, sometimes it is even dishonest. Moral idealism is not uncommonly the quest for an existence freed at last from any burden whatever: an aspiration opposed to nature which can end only in ruin, or in anti-humanity.

In this sense property, like intimacy, is a concrete requirement of personality. To exclude it for fear of its abuses is utopian, and the communists themselves, apart from a few of their sects, have never pretended to abolish it. It expresses the vocation, at once dual and integral, of the person—to be both centred in, and expansive around, himself.

Nevertheless, if having is of the substance of our being, it is also the burden of it. Beginning as a vibration of desire, the will to have presses on to triumph and the exaltation of conquest: but the victor soon becomes the vassal, the possessor of dead goods is possessed by them; in the end he can enjoy

[1] In this respect even G. Marcel goes a little too far, in his *Being and Having* (Harvill Press); *Le Journal métaphysique*; *Du Refus à l'invocation* (Gallimard).

only the prestige they give him, and may die dried-up in the desert of his riches.[1] Nor must we forget that this degradation of having begins at the heart, as a fruit rots from the core. It is not only in the historic and accidental derangements of the present customs of ownership that there is an evil, destined to disappear with the social order that produced it. At the heart of all human possessing, a corrupting influence is at work and is continually renewed. Possession, like the hand of King Midas, tends to degrade every being or object that I annex to myself, for it presents me to them in the light of a conqueror who exacts or a master who dominates, restricting at the same time both their availability and my own. People often speak of an 'expansion of personality', as though the person had only to extend its field of action to heighten its value. They commend worldly possessions as if these were intrinsically liberating. But the personalist dialectic of having is not so confident, for it sees beyond, to the entropic and involutionary function of having. Expansion of personality implies, as an interior condition, a renunciation of the self and of its goods which depolarises egocentricity; for only in losing himself can the person find himself. His riches consist in what remains with him when he is stripped of all his possessions—in what is still his in the hour of death. Not that either formal asceticism or economic malthusianism are the right conclusions to draw from these observations; we are here concerned with the disposition of the possessor and his effective use of his possessions, irrespective of their quantity. The social problems of property and its distribution are additional to the principles we are considering here, which do not pretend to be solutions.

---

[1] Cf. the fuller analysis of this dialectic in E. MOUNIER: *De la propriété capitaliste à la propriété humaine* (De Brouwer 1936) reprinted in *Liberté sous conditions* (Ed. du Seuil, 1946). Concerning this paragraph see also *Traité du caractère*, Chap. X. The critique of having is touched upon by MARX. *Economie politique et philosophie* (Ed. Molitor, especially p. 30).

Vocation

Concentrating in order to find oneself; then going forth to enrich and to find oneself again; concentrating oneself anew through dispossession; such is the systole and diastole of the personal life, an everlasting quest for a unity foretold and longed-for but never realized. I am *a* being, in the *singular*, I have a *proper* name—a unity that is not the dead identity of a stone which is neither born, nor lives nor grows old. Nor is this the unity of a whole which one can embrace in a formula. Surprises innumerable arise out of the abysses of the unconscious, out of the abysses of the super-conscious and out of the spontaneity of freedom, incessantly renewing the question of my identity. It is not presented to me as something given, like my inherited gifts or my aptitudes, nor as a pure acquisition. It is not self-evident; but neither is the unity of a picture, of a symphony, of a nation or of a narrative self-evident at a first acquaintance. One has to search oneself to find, amongst the litter of distracting motives, so much as a desire to seek this living unity, then to listen patiently for what it may whisper to one, to test it in struggle and obscurity, and even then one can never be sure that one grasps its meaning. It resembles, more than anything, a secret voice, calling to us in a language that we would have to spend our lives in learning; which is why the word 'vocation' describes it better than any other. It is a word rich in meaning to the Christian, who believes in the all-embracing appeal of one Person. But a personalist standpoint is sufficiently defined even in this thought—that the significance of every person is such that he is irreplaceable in the position he occupies in the world of persons.[1] Such is the majestic status of the person, endowing it with the dignity of a universe; and yet also its humility, for in this dignity each person is equivalent to every other, and persons are more numerous than the stars. It is obvious that

[1] Cf. *Esprit* 1st April 1938 Jean GOSSET: *Vocation et destination.*

this has nothing to do with the pseudo 'vocations' of the professions, which too often follow the bent of temperament or the prompting of the environment.

A person's continual re-interpretation of his vocation is so incessantly disruptive of every short-term objective—his own interest, adaptation or success—that in this respect one might regard the person as *arbitrariness* itself, even though his every action were one of commitment or devotion. But this arbitrariness is simply that which, in a man, cannot be made use of. Therefore, in questions of the collective life, personalism always gives the techniques of *education* and *persuasion* priority over the techniques of enforcement, diplomacy or deception; for man only works well when he is working with the whole of himself. Unity in a world of persons cannot be obtained without diversity of vocations and authenticity of membership. It is approached by a long and difficult road, not by the brutal abridgments of power; and though it would be utopian to suppose that the right route will always be maintained, it should at least control our general directives for action. Totalitarian methods proceed from the impatience of the powerful.

The dialectic of the interior and the objective

Personal existence is thus always in dispute between a movement of exteriorization and a movement of interiorization, both of which are essential to it, and by either of these it may become encysted[1] or, alternatively, dissipated.

We have already alluded to the misery of the person who has become objectified. It is from this torpor, or even death in objectivity, that the great personalist movements come to awaken us. We are often warned against the danger of becoming shut up in ourselves, and it is very real. Of the majority

[1] A biological analogy. Encystment is the process by which an organism develops an enclosing membrane or carapace to protect it from external contacts. (Trans.)

of men, however, and of a great part of our lives, thronged as they are with worldly solicitations, the truer description is that of Valéry: "We are shut up *outside* ourselves." From that kind of imprisonment nothing but contemplation can deliver us.

But within ourselves too, we encounter the same dangers both of dissipation and sclerosis, for they pursue us into our retreat. Excessive rumination dissipates us, too much interiorization leads to over-subtlety, and too much self-solicitude, however spiritual, can engender an egocentricity that grows like a psychic cancer. The cultivation of a certain image of the self in order to preserve and protect it, may then come to fill the entire horizon of a life. This may have originated in a spoiled and over-sheltered childhood; as the psychologists say, the 'acquisitive' tendencies have overcome the 'oblative', so that adaptation to others and to reality has been prejudiced from infancy. The usual outcome is a life that is never sufficiently involved in virile labour and communal discipline: perhaps the greatest evils of our epoch are those of the uprooted and the unoccupied. Ever since the 15th century Western man has been slipping slowly down this slope: every value has been devalued to please the groundlings in a theatre of Narcissus, where even the rôles of sanctity and heroism are played by glory and 'success', that of spiritual force by 'toughness'; where love is debased to eroticism, intelligence to intellectualism, reason to cunning, meditation to introspection, and the passion for truth reduced to the shallowest 'sincerities'.

It is high time, therefore, to remind the subject that he will never re-discover and strengthen himself without the mediation of the objective: *he must come out of his inwardness if he is to keep his soul alive*. The flower of first love, says Kierkegaard, withers if love will not pass through the ordeal of faithfulness (of repetition) in the institution of marriage, which, after putting love to disarray, restores it to fuller bloom. Klages has declared that there is a true instinct of exteriorization: the person is, indeed, an inside in need of an outside; and the very word 'exist' indicates by its prefix that 'to be' is to go out, to express oneself. It is this primordial motive which, in an active form, moves us to exteriorise our feelings in mimicry or in speech, to inflict the imprint of our action upon visible works and to intervene in the affairs of the world and of other people. All the dimensions of the person are mutually sustaining and constitutive. The pressure of nature upon us and the labours by which we respond to it, are not merely factors making for productivity; they are also forces disruptive of egocentricity, and for that reason they are cultural and spiritual forces, quite as important as power or riches and doubtless more so. We must not, then, undervalue the external life: without it the inner life tends to insanity, as surely as the outer life becomes chaotic without interiorization.

CHAPTER IV

CONFRONTATION

IF there are mystics of personality who sometimes 'interiorize' the person to excess, forgetting its presence and embodiment in the world, there are also politicians of the person who have so keen a consciousness of its exposed situation that they often seem to think about the person simply as military experts do of their country—of its frontiers, its defensive works, of its power of resistance to attack. Personalist language fails in that case to inspire a creative impulse, and produces a separative and defensive reaction. The 'defense of personality' sometimes provides cover for a kind of sectarian spirit which it ought to avoid.

The person discloses and explains itself, it faces life with an open countenance. The Greek word that comes nearest to our notion of the person is πρόσωπον—one who looks straight in front of himself, one who *confronts*. But it faces a hostile world: the attitude of opposition is thus implicit in its very condition—which is a pregnant source of confusion.

The singular. The exceptional

To be odd, singular, original, or to be a personality, are often almost synonymous expressions in common speech. He is a 'character', we say of someone who is a well-distinguished personality. To the well-educated opinion of our day, the prime value of personality is often its *difference* from others. This is believed to be endangered by the growing uniformity of social customs and clothing all over the world. It is true

E

enough that the person is, by definition, that which is never duplicated, not even when individuals, steeped as they commonly are in conventionality, most desperately copy and recopy each other's superficial gestures and expressions. But the cult of originality appears always as a secondary product, not to say by-product, of the personal life. A hero in the heat of battle, a lover giving himself for love, a creative artist absorbed in his work, a saint inspired by love for his God—none of these would think, at such moments of supremely personal existence, of trying to be original or unique. They are too profoundly possessed by what they are doing to consider how they are doing it in any comparative sense. Moreover, as they themselves tell us, at these altitudes of existence the experience to which they attain is a kind of sublimation of the commonplace, of the simplest realities of our common humanity. To hold one's consciousness in this intense detachment, yet to prevent its fading into the drab light of everyday, is the great difficulty of the poet writing of love or of the painter translating his vision into the visible.

For the same reason, we must avoid thinking of the highest personal life as that of the *exceptional* person attaining an inaccessible height solely by his own exertion. Personalism is not an ethic of 'great men'; nor is it a new doctrine of aristocracy, an eclecticism of all the most fascinating spiritual and psychological successes, designed for the education of solitary leaders of mankind. That, as we know, was what Nietzsche wanted, and since then plenty of coxcombs, drunk with defiance, have set up their rostrums in his name. But if personality is fulfilled in pursuit of values that extend into the infinite it is none the less called upon to discern and achieve the extraordinary in everyday life. But this is a super-ordinariness, by which a person is not set apart, for every other person is also called to it. In the words of Kierkegaard—though he, too, sometimes slipped into the temptation of extremism—"The really 'exceptional' man is the truly ordinary man."

The values of refusal. The Person as a protest

To exist is to say Yes, it is acceptance and membership. Yet always to assent and never to refuse is to sink in a quicksand. To exist personally means also, and not seldom, knowing how to say no, to protest, to break away. Jaspers has underlined the staggering question presented to every man by the ultimate negations of suicide and of mysticism, the one a negation of life itself, the other of the world. The most modest existence is still a cutting off, a de-cision. Every attachment shackles my liberty, every work burdens me with its weight, every notion even that I entertain arrests my thinking. To be a presence in the world is not easy! I am lost if I flee from it, I am also lost if I give myself up to it. It seems that I cannot preserve my freedom of manoeuvre nor, as it were, the youth of my being, except upon this condition—that I call everything in question at every moment—my beliefs, my opinions, certainties, formulas, loyalties, habits and belongings. Breakage and recoil are indeed essential categories of the personal.

However, like every other category of the personal, to isolate these is to distort them. They are dangerously emphasized by certain personalist thinkers, though not, indeed, so far as to falsify them. This over-emphasis is even more marked in the views of Heidegger and Sartre, of Kierkegaard and some of their followers, as well as in political anarchism. Why have such philosophies of refusal multiplied for the last hundred years? By all the evidence, it is because the individual feels himself to be less and less the master of his environment, which, for its part, is growing more and more highly developed and organized, and with accelerating speed, seemingly quite apart from him. The machines, the masses, the ruling powers, administration, the universe itself and its forces present themselves to him increasingly as a general menace, although in all these directions it is a generalized protection that man has been seeking. The result is a kind of social paranoia, which finds expression in philosophies and political movements, but it is rooted in a situation of maladjustment and frustration. The kind of thinking it produces usually tends to fixate the human ideal within some limited category: the romantic hero of a solitary despair or an unhappy love;[1] the political or intellectual anarchist, the refractory, the reprobate, the poetic outcast, the apocalyptic prophet, the heretic, the non-cooperator. These idealizations, unhappily, furnish many an alibi for the social misfits and spongers, the semi-lunatics, cranks and fantasists who encumber every kind of libertarian movement on the Left, every movement for 'social defence' on the Right, and heresies in every direction.

The trouble originates at different levels. On the individual-psychic plane, it generally follows upon some frustration, in childhood, of affective contact with the community, which has occurred in the course of an education either too harsh, restricted and solitary or, on the contrary, too free and easy. On the social plane, it may indicate that the community or group is one in which the human being is stifled. At a profounder level, it may express some intimate break in a person's sense of existence. Thus Kierkegaard, for whom transcendent Being and everyday existence were totally disconnected, had to reject the world to the bitter end; he refused marriage, abstained from action, refused the Church, rejected all intellectual mediation; he sought to restrict the Individual's powers of assent to a kind of solitary and paradoxical *fiat* to the Absolute. For Heidegger, to exist has nothing to do with attention to one's interior being, it is the rejection of nonentity, refusal to die. For Sartre, the human being is engulfed in a threatening, viscous state of stupidity, and can only exist by a superficial parade which keeps him from sinking in the bog. These thinkers have given us remarkable descriptions of the power to break away that is concentrated in personality. But having cleared a space in the world around them, they have nothing with which to fill it except terror, and the person as they con-

[1] Cf. Denis DE ROUGEMONT: Passion and Society (Faber, 1940).

ceive it is perpetually on the alert and the defensive. They tell us nothing of those propensities of relaxation, of receiving and of giving which are also constitutive of personal being.

Jacob's wrestling. The resort to force

It is difficult, even in philosophising, to manage the language of love with discretion, especially in the presence of sensitive souls who feel an invincible repugnance against allowing any place or any value to the use of force. What do they understand of Gandhi's cry "I would run the risk of violence a thousand times rather than permit the emasculation of a whole race."? Love is a struggle; life is a struggle against death; spiritual life is a struggle against the inertia of matter and the sloth of the body. The person attains self-consciousness, not through some ecstasy but by force of mortal combat; and force is one of its principal attributes.[1] Not the brute force of mere power and aggression, in which man forsakes his own action and imitates the behaviour of matter; but human force, which is at once internal and efficacious, spiritual and manifest. Christian moralists used to give this dimension to their conception of fortitude, and the great aim of this fortitude was to overcome the fear of bodily evil—and beyond that, of death, the supreme physical disaster. For the lack of moral courage is often, quite stupidly, a fear of being hit. Moreover, they related fortitude to liberality and magnanimity; i.e., to generosity of nature: many are made cowardly by avarice and by lack of imagination. It is always an internal victory over death that re-unites these two fields of energy: a person only comes to full maturity at the moment when he is seized of loyalties he values more than life itself. But in modern conditions of comfort and of indulgent care for the feelings, we have long cultivated, under the cover of philosophies of love and of peace, the most monstrous misunderstandings of these elementary truths. There is no society, order or right which does not originate in struggle

[1] *Eloge de la force. Esprit* February 1933.

49

between forces, or is not sustained by some force. Rights themselves are an always precarious effort to rationalize force and incline it towards the rule of love. But they are also a battle. To pretend that they are not leads nowhere but to hypocrisy: we then say we are 'against the class-struggle' as though there were any social progress without struggle: or we are 'against violence', as though we were not taking advantage of deeds of 'white violence' from morning till night, as if we were not always participating at a distance in a sort of diffused murder of mankind. Utopia, projected as a state of repose and harmony, as a 'state of abundance', a 'reign of law', a 'realm of liberty', or of 'perpetual peace', is an aspiration that may sustain man in his infinite and endless labour. But let us not degrade it into a puerile fantasy.

The real problem for us, who are engaged 'for the duration' of the human struggle between opposing forces, is that we are required by our vocation to fight at the same time against the *rule* of force, and against the establishment of vested interests in force. In striving to prevent a reign of universal violence, certain absolute prophetic negations doubtless have their place. But in general, personal life necessitates the confrontation of violence by violence; to try to eradicate aggressiveness altogether from education, or too early to swamp the virile energies of youth in idealistic hopes—this is less likely to realize any ideal than to spoil the fighters for it.

Affirmation. *The person in acting and choosing*

To be, as we have said, is to love. But to be is also to affirm oneself. From whatever standpoint we attempt an objective study of the self, whether we subordinate its spiritual reality to its physical determinants, or its physical reality to its spiritual character, the one thing we can never demonstrate is the act by which it calls itself *I*. This elementary *datum* of experience in mutual communication is not even the most subtle nor the most universal state of mind that we can imagine, but is an act by which, in expressing, I also affirm myself. This act, apparently so simple, is the product of a complex culture and of a delicate equilibrium. The capacity for it is but slowly acquired in childhood, it is toughened in the gradual growth of ego-centrality, it is liable to distortion by greed and pride, and it founders altogether in certain psychic catastrophes. My biological and sexual equilibrium contribute to it no less than the way in which I adapt myself to my surroundings, or the moral judgment I pronounce upon myself in the intimacy of my own conscience. The person, however richly endowed, may break down, or may break itself.

But to act is to choose, which means to decide, to cut short; and in adopting one course of procedure to reject another. As Nédoncelle says, the realm of liberty has its housing problem. There is still something infantile in the mentality of those people who will never exclude anything or hurt anyone, who think that their inability to select is comprehensiveness, and that the resulting confusion is openness of mind. To cultivate means to sacrifice. Not that to decide is a blind and arbitrary deed of internal violence. It is a movement of the whole person, at one with the future, focused upon some act of difficulty but of promise, which integrates the person and his experience in a fresh experience.

The rejections thus necessitated are indeed renunciations, embarrassing or even acutely painful; but they are not mutilations. Dictated by an imperious plenitude of being, they do not impoverish. They are moreover creative. Every organization, every technique, every doctrine which tends to deny or diminish this fundamental vocation of the person to exercise responsible choice, whatever advantages it may offer, is a poison more dangerous than despair.

The Irreducible

Though these negations, these moments in which the person says No, are more often than not dialectical and imply a recuperation, there always comes a moment when refusal is irreducible, because the very being of the person is at stake.

There is one indomitable passion in personality, forever burning within it like a sacred fire, that is fanned into flame by any wind that smells of servitude, rousing the person to defend, rather than life itself, the dignity of life. This is the mark of the free man, the incorruptible—the man who, as Bernanos says, 'is able to impose discipline upon himself, but will not take it blindly from anyone else; the man who finds his "comfort" in doing, as far as possible, what he wills, at what time he chooses, even though he must pay with solitude or poverty for the interior voice whose approval he holds beyond all price; the man who may give himself, or may refuse himself, but who will never lend himself.'

This is a rare species. Men in the mass prefer servitude in security to the risks of independence, a material and vegetative existence to the human adventure. Nevertheless, the revolt against tyranny, the resistance to oppression, the refusal to accept humiliation, all represent the inalienable right of the person, its last resort when the world proceeds in disregard of its sovereignty. It is right that the ruling powers should define and defend the fundamental rights and guarantees of personal life; its corporal and moral immunity from systematic violence, from degrading treatment, material or mental privation, collective suggestion and propaganda. They ought to assure liberty of movement, of speech and writing, of association and of education; the rights of private life and of the home; *habeas corpus;* the presumption of innocence until culpability has been proved; the protection of labour, of the public health, of race, of sex, of old age and retirement. But the frontiers where these rights have to be adjusted to the good of society as a whole will forever be in dispute. The most solemn declarations of Rights are speedily transgressed in a state that contains too few men of indomitable character to confirm them, or social structures too weak to guarantee their realization. Any society in which the governments, the press and the leaders of opinion are disseminating little but scepticism, trickery and submissiveness is a society that is dying; it is only moralising in order to dissimulate its decay.

CHAPTER V

FREEDOM UNDER CONDITIONS

Freedom has plenty of friends. Liberals regard themselves as its commissioned champions, while the Marxists, with whom they dispute this title, claim to be bringing about the true 'reign of liberty' beyond and in despite of the liberal illusion. To existentialists and Christians, too, freedom is the essence of their endeavours, which however differ from one another and from both the others. Why so much confusion? Because, as soon as one isolates freedom from the whole structure of the person, it tends towards some aberration.

Freedom is not any thing

Without freedom, what are we but the sport of the universe? Such a thought is insupportable, and to escape from it we resort to illegal appropriation, flagrantly seize upon freedom as an object, or at the least seek to prove it as a theorem; we try to establish that *there is some* freedom *in the world*—but in vain. Freedom is the affirmation of the person, it can be lived, but not seen. The objective world presents us with nothing but objects that are given, and situations that are occurring. Since we can find no place in this world for freedom, we look for it in a negative form—an absence of cause, a hiatus in the sequence of determinism: but what can we make of a negation? At the best we can only discern, not indeed in nature but at the natural level, two forms in which freedom may possibly exist.

One is the freedom of indifference: freedom to be nothing, to wish for nothing and to do nothing; not merely indeterminism but total indetermination. There are liberals, and some anarchist thinkers, who conceive freedom of thought or of action in this way. But a man never in fact experiences the required state of equipoise. By persuading him to believe that this is possible, one can only conceal from him the real options he has; one may even induce in him a fatal liking for indifference.

The alternative is to beg the question from the physicists' abandonment of strict causality. Much has been made of this transformation in the outlook of modern physics, which many have wished to misappropriate as a 'proof of free-will'. But this is making nonsense of free-will. Human freedom cannot be a 'remainder' after adding up the sum of matter. If freedom were merely an irregularity in the working of the universe, who could prove that it was not reducible to a defect in our perception, or even to some systematic distortion in nature or in man? What can I profit from such a defect? The indeterminism of modern physics calls the bluff of the positivists, but it does no more. Freedom is not to be realised in despite of natural causes: it is won from them, but also with them.

All that can be said about this development is that—

(1) Modern science finds it cannot explain all the customs of matter upon the principle of causality, which is the kind of explanation it used to look for: and this conclusion has emerged from those of its activities (mathematics and logistics) which were expected to lead science straight towards systematic certainty. If science has nothing to add in favour of freedom, it is being forced, more and more, to give up denying freedom.

(2) Nature discloses a slow but sure development of conditions favourable for freedom. The fact that the unit of matter is not determined is no proof of freewill, but it does suggest the non-rigid structure of a universe in which freedom is operative. The living molecule does not demon-

strate freedom, but such an accumulation of explosive energy makes no sense unless it represents a multiplication of possibilities and a preparation for centres of choice. The achievement by the animal kingdom of that autonomy over great physiological systems which enables the individual to regulate its nutrition, its warmth, its movements and its intercourse with others—this again is not freedom, but it is a preparation for the physical autonomy which can express the spiritual autonomy of the free human being.

Nevertheless, freedom does not grow out of such preparations as the fruit grows out of the flower. Amongst all the enigmatic natural forces in which these preparations are involved and embroiled, it is the irreplaceable initiative of the person alone that can discern openings conducive to its freedom, enter and exploit them. It is the person that makes itself free, having first chosen to be so; but nowhere does it find freedom given or instituted: nor does anything in the world assure it of freedom unless it enters courageously into free experience.

Freedom is not pure spontaneity

Seeing that freedom is not a thing, some people deny that it is objective in any sense whatever. Objective being (Sartre's 'being in itself') is self-identical and changeless; if lasting, it repeats itself indefinitely. On the other hand, free existence would be an incessant change of quality, a fount of originality (the *Ursprung* of the Germans), a perpetual invention of the self by the self; in other words, absolute subjectivity. One could only grasp it *from within* and *by the roots*, in the act of being free.

If freedom were in truth this absolute affirmation, nothing would be able to limit it: it would be whole and unconfined (Sartre) by the mere fact that it existed. It could not express the nature of anything anterior to it, or respond to any appeal, for if it did so it would not be free. It makes itself, and in making itself it makes me: in it and by it I invent myself, I invent my motives, my values and my world as well as myself, without any support or assistance.

Such absolute freedom is a myth.

Our notion of nature may be confused, and in need of clarification. But it does express the fact that existence is not only ever-renewed; that it has, at the same time, continuity and density; it is not only recreated but given. I am not only what I do, and my world is not simply what I will. I am something *given* to myself and the world existed before me. Such being my condition, my liberty itself is qualified by a number of factors—some arising out of myself, the limitations of my individual being; others inherent in the world, the necessities that restrict and the values that direct my liberty. Indeed, my freedom lies in a field of well-nigh universal gravitation. To forget this is only to subtilize the facts into a kind of shadow, an idea without consistency, a dream-limit; something shapeless but felt as absolute. This can excite the individual to alternate somersaults of revolt and exaltation, by the sheer intensity of which he is captivated, while remaining indifferent to their contradictions (this is the universe of Malraux or of de Montherlant).

There is a still graver consequence. A freedom that gushes forth as sheer reality, that is so closely involved with the crude assertion of existence that it is presented as a necessity—Sartre calls it a condemnation—is a blind force of nature, a naked power. Who will distinguish it from instinctive preference and from the will to power? How can it be mine, if I cannot refuse it? Where will this freedom take on a human countenance, if the face of man is formed only by his own decisions? Who will keep it within human bounds, if the only frontiers between the human and inhuman are those that it decrees? Or who will restrain this freedom from desiring, in some supreme exaltation, to experience its own dissolution? From this position we are in peril of drifting not only towards the illusions of formalized liberty, but into the frenzies of 'living intensely'. Whoever feels himself 'condemned' to freedom, to an absurd and illimitable liberty, may find no distraction from his fate except in condemning others to it, like Caligula, by sheer terrorism. But freedom is not branded upon personal being like a condemnation, it is offered as a gift. It can be accepted or refused, and the free man is he who can promise or who can betray (G. Marcel). He is no slave of his freedom, no drug-addict of liberty, nor will he contaminate the freedom of others with any taint of servitude whatsoever.

In a world in which every freedom arose in isolation from all others, what would finally become of the community of persons? "I cannot truly be free," wrote Bakunin, "until everyone around me, man or woman, is equally free. . . . I become free only through the liberty of others." That is a true saying: the demand for my own liberty is too much mixed with instinct to be above suspicion; and it has been rightly said that the sense of freedom begins with a feeling for the liberty of others.[1] Such a co-operation between freedoms would be excluded if, as Sartre thinks, no one were able to unite his own freedom with that of another without one of the two being dominant and the other subservient.

Freedom of that kind, rooted in an inward necessity, can only communicate necessity. It does not liberate those that it touches, at the best it can but drag them out of their sleep, only to draw them into its own ineluctable whirlpool. The freedom of the person, on the other hand, creates freedom around itself by a sort of contagious sanity—as surely as, conversely, deranged minds tend to engender derangement in others about them.

Freedom in the total environment of the person

It remains true, nevertheless, that freedom is the life and source of personal being, and that an action is less than human

[1] Et. de GREEFF: *Notre Destinée et nos instincts*.

unless it transfigures the most obstinate data by the magic of its spontaneity. In this sense, but in this sense only, man is altogether and always free within himself whenever he wants to be so. Such freedom remains to the convict, even at the moment when he seems to be wholly subjected and humiliated. In this sense, one may also assert that concrete liberties are not indispensable to the exercise of spiritual freedom; the very lack of them may enable a man to manifest, in certain moments of greatness, his transcendence of all factual conditions.

Yet human freedom is the freedom of *a person*, moreover of *this person*, thus and thus constituted, situated in the world and in the presence of definite values.

This implies that it is strictly conditioned and delimited by the common laws of our concrete situation. To be free is, in the first place, to accept this position and base oneself upon it. Not everything is possible, or not everything at any moment. These limitations, when not actually cramping, are points of vantage: freedom grows like the body, by means of obstacles, by the exercise of choice and by the sacrifices that it entails. The idea of free will is however linked with the idea of fullness of life; and in too restrictive conditions freedom may amount to hardly more than what Marx called 'the awareness of necessity'. That indeed, is its beginning, for such a consciousness holds the promise and the spring of liberating activity (he who is blind to his servitude is the only real slave, even if he be a happy one). It is but the beginning of freedom and is only just human. But before we seek to establish freedom through constitutions or make orations about it, we had better assure those *common* conditions of biological, economic, social and political freedom which put average minds in a position to respond to the highest appeals of humanity; we need therefore to be as careful of specific *liberties* as of general *freedom*. Indiscriminately to defend 'freedom', otherwise undefined, when and wherever social customs or reasons of state set bounds to it, is to range oneself on the side of the static, and against the moving, forces of mankind. The liberties of yester-day are always being broken into by the liberties of tomorrow; the liberties of the nobility were menaced by those of the bourgeoisie; those of the bourgeoisie are threatened by those of the populace; the freedom of all may compromise that of the few. It is thus possible, as Marx wrote, for the noblest Declarations of Rights to cloak, by their very generality, the sole liberty 'of egotistic man, of man divided from man and from the community'.

It is these falsifications that have kept the banner of 'Freedom' flapping in contrary winds for over a century. At one and the same time, from 1820 to 1830, freedom was in-voked, upon the spiritual and intellectual plane, by Christian traditionalists such as Montalembert against the modern centralised and secular State of the Napoleonic bureaucracy; upon the economic plane by the rising bourgeoisie, clamouring to get elbow room for their vast new industrial enterprises; and upon the political plane by popular leaders and the precur-sors of socialism. Bourgeois liberty had established its rights by the reign of Louis-Philippe, and asked for no more; whilst the people let themselves be persuaded that the liberties of their masters were also theirs. For Montalembert, too, freedom was saved. But as popular opinion hardened after 1830 and exploded all over Europe in 1848, Montalembert and the Voltairian bourgeoisie abandoned political liberty without regrets, in order to safeguard their economic and social privi-leges; and the national-industrial Emperor was a prelude, in a minor key, to the future national-socialist democracy. His reign drove the cause of freedom back to the Left, where it re-mained throughout the high summer of political Liberalism. So long as the liberals were satisfied with enlargements of their own privileges, their notion of freedom grew more conservative in opposition to socialism, but later there was division in their ranks. Some remained liberal both in their sympathies and antipathies, but others did not hesitate, when the period of fascism began, to sacrifice political liberty in the hope of salvaging their world. There has been a corresponding fission on the Left since Lenin, which has widened since Stalin, dividing the liberal democrats and socialists from a fully authoritarian socialism; for the latter is ready to sacrifice every political freedom to the necessity of an economic liberation that is to be completed by the disappearance of all political restraint. Since then freedom has been invoked no less wildly by the Left (anti-fascist liberty) than by the Right (anti-communist liberalism).

But if our freedom is that of the person *in its situation*, it is also that of a person realising *values*. I am not set free simply by the exercise of my spontaneity; I only become free in so far as this spontaneity moves towards human liberation—that is, towards the personalization of myself and of my world. We have here another aspect of the movement of life towards freedom, another distinction between the implicit personality, still within the fringes of natural vitality, and the personality as it is matured by action in a widening life of individual and collective experience. Thus my freedom is never at my arbitrary disposal, although the point at which I espouse it may be hidden in the heart's most secret depth. My liberty is never mere spontaneity: it is always something regulated—better still, it is something called forth.

It is this *call* which gives freedom its spiritual force and that is why, upon an inadequate analysis, it is apt to be confused with the *impulse* to freedom. For if the call fades, the free spirit relapses, adapts itself. Adaptation is necessary, but to adapt oneself too well is to become enmeshed and finally immobile. We need, for instance, to understand historical necessity in order to insert our own action into it; but if we hold too tightly to history as it has been, we soon cease to make history what it ought to be. We need to study the nature of man; but by too carefully defining its known forms, we may cease to develop its unexplored possibilities: that is what happens to every

F

kind of conformist. In exercising his freedom man needs to be modest, but also intrepid. The evasive attitude of the public confronted by the strenuous demands of today is frequently denounced; but in an epoch intimidated by so much that it accepts as fatality, and so undermined by care and anxiety that it is ready to give up its liberties for a minimum of security, it is no less necessary to denounce the spirit of servitude, and to nip it in the bud. A kind of passive hankering for authority, which springs from pathological rather than theological roots, a blind adherence to party lines and the docile indifference of the bewildered masses, all show that the free man is in retreat, his forces in need of reorganization. Freedom is a practical need, but also a divine imperative; and must be not only directed against the stubbornness of the material but allowed its never-ending aspirations, even its moments of creative folly. The love of freedom, it is true, should never forget particular liberties. But men who cease to dream of cathedrals will not long know how to build good villas; and those who have lost the passion for freedom become incapable of protecting concrete liberties. Freedom cannot be given to men from outside, like the social services or a reformed Constitution; they only drop asleep upon such liberties and wake up as enslaved as before. Our *liberties* can be no more than opportunities offered to the *spirit of freedom*.

The spirit of freedom is indefatigable in tracing and regaining lost liberties—i.e., in dealing with situations in which one is delivered up like an object to the play of impersonal forces. A number of such situations has been described by the Marxists (though there are others which they quite misunderstand). The conditions of our existence are such that there is no human situation without a more or less definite alienation of freedom: it is the nature of man's lot that he should aspire for ever to autonomy, pursue it ceaselessly, yet fail indefinitely of its attainment. For man to be altogether insured against any loss of his freedom, nature would have to be completely intelligible, communion would have to be continuous, universal and perfect, and man in possession of all his ideals. Even from the alienations of liberty that occur in history and endure but for a time, there is no respite: as soon as one is overcome another arises; each new victory for freedom is turned against it and demands another battle: the struggle for freedom knows no end.

Freedom of choice and freedom of association

Each stage of the combat is marked and consolidated by what Kierkegaard called the 'baptism of choice'. Choice appears first of all as a power in him who chooses. When I choose this and not that I am indirectly choosing myself, edifying (building-up) myself by the decision. By having dared, by having exposed myself, by having taken the risk in obscurity and uncertainty, I have found something more of myself, which I was not actually looking for. The creative decision, by breaking a chain of probabilities or fatalities, or braving an intimidating play of forces, has upset all calculation: it was taken in conditions of uncertainty and confusion, but it becomes the creative origin of a new state of order and intelligibility. The world progresses and man forms himself by this alone. No technical organization will ever replace it; on the contrary, the more technique we contrive, the more freedom of decision will be required of us.

However, a sort of philosophic myopia tends to see the centre and pivot of freedom in the act of choice, whereas it lies in progressive liberation to choose the good. What would be the value of freedom merely to choose between the plague and cholera? And if men today are becoming indifferent to freedom, may it not be that they no longer know what to do with freedom? Freedom enchants us indeed by a beauty of its own, by its godlike dignity, but it would not reflect that beauty of sovereign being unless it were also a power to our salvation. To fix one's attention upon freedom as no more than the ability to choose is to slacken the will to freedom, and soon renders one impotent to choose for lack of any adequate motive: it is to promote that cult of abstention and alternation which is one of the spiritual maladies of the contemporary mind. To put the case for freedom as merely the achievement of autonomy moreover encourages that contraction of individuality which makes the individual opaque and incommunicative. The movement of freedom also includes relaxation, receptiveness, preparedness and availability; it is not only refusal and conquest, but it is also—and ultimately —the act of association. The free man is the man to whom the world puts questions and who responds accordingly; he is the *responsible* man. Freedom of this kind is a unitive force, not a divisive one, and far from tending to anarchy, it is, in the original sense of the words, religious and devoted. Freedom is not the being of the person, but the mode and manner in which the person is everything that it is, and the more fully because it is freely so. But with these conclusions, we arrive at yet another essential aspect of the nature of the person.

CHAPTER VI

THE HIGHEST DIGNITY

Is there some reality beyond that of personality? Certain personalist authors, including MacTaggart, Renouvier and Howison reply in the negative. For Jaspers, personal reality presupposes an inner transcendence, but this transcendent being is nameless and inaccessible, except in a kind of mathematical language. From our present point of view, however, the movement that constitutes personality does not remain enclosed within itself, but relates to something transcendent dwelling amongst us; nor does this escape all attempts to describe it.

Concrete approaches to the transcendent

We have seen that, in thinking of the transcendent, we have to beware of spatial images. A reality that transcends another is not one that is separated from and floating above it, but a reality that is superior in the quality of its being. Nor can the reality that it transcends attain to it gradually and continuously without a hiatus, a leap in dialectic and in expression. Since spiritual relationships are those of intimate distinction, not of external juxtaposition, the relation of transcendence does not exclude the transcendent reality from being present in the heart of him whom it transcends: as St. Augustin said, God is closer to me than my own thoughts.

The transcendent in the person manifests itself at once in its productive activity. 'To make, in making to make oneself, and to be nothing but what one has made oneself'—this formula, in which Sartre wants to comprehend the whole of man, is very nearly the Marxian one. But production is no such solitary task. Matter itself overflows with the unexpected and overwhelms my efforts. The producer, for his part, is not sufficient unto himself: productive work that is purposeless soon turns into a torture (as some deported prisoners have found by experience). Every attempt to reduce all, including spiritual, activity to that of construction and fabrication finally breaks down in the face of certain fundamental human realities:—e.g., the receptive element in knowledge, wonder, affirmation (G. Marcel), the irrational (Meyerson), and the intentional (Husserl).

In affirming myself, however, I feel that my most deeply-motivated and my most highly creative actions surge up from within, as it were unawares. My freedom itself comes to me as something given: its supreme moments are not those in which I exercise most will-power; they are moments rather of giving-way, or of offering myself to a freedom newly encountered or to a value that I love.

This *surpassing* of the self must not be confused with the breaking-out of the vital impulses: the life-force never prompts us to anything *other* than itself; it is the passion for life at any price, even at the cost of the values that give life its meaning. To accept suffering and death in order not to betray human values—this or any other heroic sacrifice is, on the contrary, the supreme act of the person. Such acceptance begins, as Gabriel Marcel has written, at the moment when I become aware that 'I am more than my life'. Such is the paradox of man's existence: he can find himself (on the personal plane) only by losing himself (upon the biological plane). 'I love those', said Nietzsche,[1] 'who do not know how to live except in perishing, for it is they who are going beyond man.'

Nor is this a question of what is sometimes called social impulse, of a movement which impels us continually to widen

[1] In *Thus Spake Zarathrustra* Part I (introductory) Section 4.

our social contacts. For this, as Bergson has shown, tends to its own contradiction by forming closed societies, where the self entrenches itself in a kind of aggrandised egoism. Nor does the aspiration of the person to transcend itself appear in any kind of agitation, but in a denial of the selfhood which would shut it up in an autarkic world of its own, dependent upon its isolated will. The person is not absolute being, but a movement of being towards itself, and has consistency only in the being that it is moving towards. Without that aspiration it would disintegrate (v. Müller-Frienfels) into 'momentary subjectivities'.

The interior richness of personal being endows it with a continuity, not of repetition but of super-abundance. The person cannot be inventoried.[1] It is felt as something that overflows any conception meant to contain it. Physical modesty means that one's body is more than a body; social reserve signifies that one is more than one's words and gestures; irony that the idea is more than an idea. In perception, thought corrects the senses; in thought faith overrules fatality, even as action overrules the volitions that suggested it, and as love disciplines the desires that it awakens. Man, as Malebranche said, is a movement that is always going further yet. Personal being is essentially generous. Thus, the order that it founds is the converse of adaptation and security. For to adapt oneself is to shorten the line, to reduce the exposed flank, to assimilate oneself to what is, at the cost of what could be. The life within us asks nothing better, especially in the face of danger, than adaptation at the cheapest price, and is very willing to strike a bargain: but the person is always risking and spending, without counting the cost.

The Aim of the Transcendent

Is this overflow of the personal being directed toward an end? The continual projecting of itself, upon the screen of the

[1] See p. 35 *ante*. (G. Marcel).

future, by a being without purpose in a universe without meaning would be no sort of orientation, still less a true transcendence. When the person surpasses itself, it does so by what is not merely a pro-ject, but an elevation (Jaspers). The personal being is made for a movement that exceeds itself: like the bicycle or the aeroplane which can only keep their balance by moving at more than a certain speed, man can only keep spiritually upright at more than a certain minimum rate of ascent. If he 'loses height' man does not descend to some average human level, nor, as many suppose, to the animal level, but to something much lower. No living being except man has invented such cruelties and meannesses as man practises to this day.

But what is the goal of this movement of transcendence? Jaspers refuses to name it. Several contemporary thinkers speak of 'values', conceived as realities in themselves apart from their relations, and recognizable *à priori* (Scheler, Hartmann). Personalists however cannot willingly surrender the person to anything impersonal, and most of them seek in one way or another to personalize these values. Christian personalism goes the whole way, and deduces all values from the unique appeal of the one supreme Person.

We may be asked for evidence of the transcendent, for proofs of the value of these values; but the transcendent, being inherent in the universe of freedom, is not susceptible of proof. Its verification is manifested in the fullness of the personal life. Alternatively, it is obscured by failure of personal life, for then the subject may become blind to value, and his ontological disillusion may turn into hatred.

The Personalization of Values

Even faith in a personal God avails itself of mediations that appear impersonal; of notions of goodness, omnipotence, justice, of moral and spiritual law, etc. These values, however, are wholly different from general ideas, although, in a kind of mental frailty, we are prone to use them as such. A general idea is a selected sum of determinate ideas, and its potency is that of repetition only: e.g., the quadruped is any animal with four legs. But a value is a living and inexhaustible source of determinations, an exuberance and radio-activity of ideas: and in this it exhibits a kind of expansive singularity, a relationship with personal being that is primordial, which is obscured when it is allowed to lapse into a generalization.

Moreover, a value tends irresistibly towards embodiment in a concrete subject, either individual or collective.

Of these the most enduring are the realities of history. These appear successively in the consciousness of humanity in the course of its evolution, as though the vocation of each succeeding age of the human race were to discover or to invent for the others a new species of values. One may speak of the vocation of an epoch or of a nation; of honour as a mediaeval value, or of liberty or social justice as modern values. Or, in terms of space rather than time, compassion is an Indian value, grace a French value, community is Russian, and so on. Each of these is born, develops, becomes ossified and then passes into obscurity or a kind of historic latency. Whilst it is becoming ossified, it is a source of misunderstanding. A vigorous defender of the family, of freedom or of socialism may be further from the spirit of these values than another person who seems to be opposing them, but in fact is only incensed against the hardened and decadent forms they have assumed. Even eternal values are, contrary to common prejudice, the reverse of immobile, they reappear continually in a new guise. To try to fix a value in one of its historic forms, when its decline has just set in, is to betray that value under pretext of preserving it.

History, however, tends to reduce values to their generalizations. Their authentic existence is in the hearts of living persons. Persons cannot in the full sense exist apart from values, but neither can any value exist except in so far as a person says to it *fiat veritas tua*. Values do not constitute a ready-made world functioning automatically, as some idle mythologists of 'the invincible power of truth' or 'the irresistible march of progress' have imagined. Values are not assignable to reality as if they were constitutive principles of it. They are revealed in the void of freedom, they mature with the motive that chose them, and they are often of a humble and lowly origin—an interest, or even a mistake—which they refine or correct in course of time.

Thus we see how ambiguous it is either to affirm or to deny that values are 'subjective'. They are not subjective, inasmuch as they are independent of the peculiarities of a given subject, but they are subjective in the sense that they exist only in relation to subjects, that they have to be re-born through persons, yet without being bound to any one of them, mediating between all, drawing them out of their isolation and relating them to the universal. Values are not to be confused with projections of the self, which so soon exhaust its limited resources. On the contrary, they are signs that a person is not a localized and separate entity, tied to a given position like a horse hobbled to a post; that he is able to survey the universe from the angle of his own position, and indefinitely to lengthen the bonds by which he is attached to it. The person could therefore be defined as a movement towards a transpersonal condition which reveals itself in the experience of community and of the attainment of values at the same time.

The two kinds of experience are indeed inseparably united. The Jansenist formula of 'the soul alone with God', which is a falsification of religious life, is no less false for the realization of any value whatever. It is true that no absolute relation to an absolute is to be achieved amidst the noises of the crowd; but if retreat is essential for this, its perfection is also attainable only by the collaboration, partly conscious and partly invisible, of many individual meditations, each being amplified and corrected by all.

This ascent of the person towards the transpersonal is a combative movement. It is in the attempt to reduce it to sheer idiosyncratic exaltation that so much idealism and spirituality becomes nauseous. Experience demonstrates that there is no value that is not born of conflict or established without struggle, from political order to social justice, from sexual love to human unity or, for Christians, to the Kingdom of God. Violence must be condemned, but to evade it at any cost is to renounce all the principal tasks of mankind.[1] Only when the value of communication has been realized can the subject know the peace that arises from the depths; and even then not perfectly, since value can never be grasped and communicated in all its fullness. In order to convey values the poet, the painter or the philosopher may have to avail himself of means that are partly obscure or disconcerting: the meaning of history remains still ambiguous; the profoundest truths can be approached only by the stratagems of myth, of paradox, of humour or translation into art: sometimes, as if in a last desperate attempt to conjure communication, he may resort even to defiance or imprecation. Yet God remains silent; all that is of value in the world is steeped in silence.

Upon these little-frequented ways, where it is so easy to play with lights and shadows, self-deception and imposture flourish in abundance. Nevertheless, out of this region shines 'the supreme dignity of man'. Respect for the human person is only secondarily respect for human life: in itself, respect for life may be no more than the instinctive will to live; it may be merely the refusal, projected and ennobled, either to kill or suppress one's repugnance to being killed. But to desire life at all costs is, some day, to buy life at the price of all reason for living. We have no authentic existence until we have an interior stronghold of values or of devotion, against which we do not believe that the fear of death itself could prevail. And

[1] P. RICOEUR: *L'Homme non-violent et sa présence à l'histoire. Esprit,* Février, 1949.

it is because they disarm these inner citadels of man that the modern techniques of degradation—financial trickery, bourgeois complaisance and political intimidation—are more deadly than weapons of war.

It remains only to indicate, in a cursory survey, the general scale of values and their bearing upon the personal life.

(1) *Happiness*. The exceptional—one may well say the abnormal—importance assumed today by the biological values, such as health and life, and those of economics, such as utility and organization, proceeds from the fact that they are compromised; for once these values are in jeopardy the whole social organism may be dislocated. We need not overestimate the rank of these values in order to acknowledge this present emergency. A man has, as a general rule, to be rescued from physiological and social misery before he can attain to the higher values: and the pharisaism that chides him for neglect of such values without giving him the most elementary means for their cultivation must be condemned. But the most perfect provision for vital and economic values, which is so generally recommended today in the name of happiness, cannot be the supreme value. We can see, from the study of the societies that are the happiest from this point of view, into what spiritual torpor they can decline—or into what storms of grief or panic folly when they think themselves endangered. Happiness then appears, in itself, to be inextricably bound up with individual egotism and the collective machine; and, either by peace at any price or by the nationalization of happiness, it seduces man to barter freedom for security, which is the reversal of the progress of mankind; or worse still, it points man down the slippery path of treason.

(2) *Science*. After happiness, science has been the leading ideal of the last two centuries. One would think that science, studying the universe and man as it does simply from the

standpoint of objective determinacy, would be a powerful dissolvent of personal realities. But in fact science never grasps these realities, and is a danger to them only when, speaking out of turn, it presumes to deny them. If that temptation is resisted, the scientific clarification of myths, of prejudices and instinctive convictions can furnish an important, though doubt-less only a preliminary stage of personal *ascesis*. Moreover, if the movement of objectification is an essential part of the total movement of our existence, there is no valid reflection which does not give full weight to scientific thinking. One of the weaknesses of existentialism is that it too often carries on its analyses as though science did not exist.

(3) *Truth. Sketch of a personalist theory of knowledge.* Certain rationalist philosophies make fictive use of a world—of nature or of ideas—which is not a world *present* to anybody, but is pure spectacle without spectator; the truth of this world is not true *for* anybody; there is no human freedom to which its truth calls or which responds to it. Before such an impersonal Reason the person is reduced to a limited point of position, destined to disappear (Spinoza, Lagneau, Brunschvicg). Moving and cogent as these philosophies may be, with their passion for universality and the discipline they apply to the deceptions of subconscious egotism, the universality to which they aspire is not that of a world of persons. They tend towards two kinds of error, equally mortal. Either they eliminate the spectator altogether as a free personal existence in order to uphold the pre-eminence of the idea—in which case an ideology becomes a power extrinsic to personality, and frequently a means of governing the spirit—or they leave us with only an 'objective' spectator, one who explains all things, under-stands all things, and admits everything. This is the internal weakness in liberalism; the source of a disintegration which constructive thinking alone is too insubstantial to arrest.

But is this to say that objectivity is without value? Tha

was the final position of Nietzsche, and since his day of all the subsequent theorists (and practioners) of irrational violence whose record would amply suffice to restore our preference, had we lost it, for reason and its disciplines. But there is no case for dethroning reason and crowning instinct; what we need is to become conscious of the global situation of the knowing being.

Outside of a limited sector of scientific definitions (which 'science' in its practical activities has surpassed) the knowing spirit is not a neutral mirror, nor is it a factory of concepts valid for personality in general; it is something that exists indissolubly linked with a body and a history, called to a destiny, and involved in the situation by all its actions, including its acts of knowledge. In each of these acts it renews itself, and, by its renewal, amplifies the meaning of what it does. Because man *is* always thus engaged in and with the situation, the involvement of the knowing subject, far from being an obstacle to true knowledge is an indispensable means to it. Truth makes no automatic or authoritarian impact upon the person; the person cannot accept it unless it is, so to speak, discreetly proposed; and truth only gives itself to those who offer themselves to it, body and soul. An intelligence which tries to reduce truth to logical formalities ends in self-destruction. Thus, in a universe of persons, truth is always something appropriated, not simply by a rational technique but by *conversion*, which is a condition prior to illumination. (One may here compare Plato's allegory of the cave, the notion of μετανοια in Christian philosophy, and those of 'uprootedness' and of 'the leap' in the existentialists.)

Yet for all this, truth is not subjective. The slippery incline on which existentialist thought is balancing itself is the liability to prefer the emotional intensity of the knowing subject to the objective value of truth. From thence to the subjective primacy of temperament, of zeal or the will-to-power, is the open road that has been taken by Nietzsche and others after him. The transcendence of values, the needs of communication and even the continuity of the personality in time, all imply, as we have seen, the recognition of objectivity. The impersonal is, viewed at this level, a way of approach to the suprapersonal; and a thorough-going personalism should be ready to correct any excessive subtilizations of the subjective by delivering, from this angle, a sound eulogy of the impersonal. Its *mediation* is our servitude, but is also our salutary discipline. A complete logic needs to be formulated upon this basis.[1] The classical systems of logic are those of the impersonal, in which judgment is applied by generalizations (Peter is good, wise, active etc.). Shutting individuals up in such classes, this logic is unable to express communication between them ("Peter is Joan"), so it either disregards or objectifies the subject. Nor can a personalist logic be a logic of pure identity, for 'self-surpassing' introduces negation and anguish into the subject, ambivalence and tension between opposing aims. True, these conflicts may be overruled by the internal pilot whose task is to maintain the faith through the dark nights of the soul; but not without painful renunciations, dictated by the saving logic of implication and of dialectical synthesis. Phases of negation and of self-withdrawal, which have to be watched lest they harden into sterile irony, are succeeded by phases of enlightenment, commitment and of profound confidence, but the very richness of this reward, brings in its turn another risk; the stifling of the spirit through indecision. Again the person must cut itself free, drive out and reject—and so on.

There are three dangers in this dialectical process: its fixation as an automatic mechanism, objective and objectifying, can kill the creative principle of personality; its arrest at the moment of alternation may make it a principle of hesitancy; or it can be corrupted by eclecticism. To confound the search for such

[1] A sketch of this is to be found in NEDONCELLE: *La personne humaine et la nature* (P.U.F.); E. MOUNIER: *Traité du caractère* 684 s., and in the work of M. BLONDEL

a logic with possible caricatures of it is however insincere criticism, although to be put upon our guard against them is always opportune. People who believe that the sheer weight of immediate affirmation, whether of subjective passion or of external authority, is what gives the most strength to individuals or to the causes they espouse, are mistaken about the very constitution of the human universe.

(4) *Moral values. Outline of a personalist ethics.* Freedom and value: the personal universe defines the moral universe and coincides with it. What is excluded from it is not immorality. Wrong doing and the state of sin are the effect and the condition of freedom. It is the pre-moral state, that of self-abandonment to the impersonal automatisms of instinct or habit, to dispersion, egocentrism, to moral indifference and blindness. Between these two states, a mystified morality tries to find, in external conformity, either a compromise between the demands of ethical values and the amoral forces, or mere masks for immorality.

Moral evil begins with these impostures. The perversion of moral values that they represent is so profound that it can no more be cured by the objective knowledge of good and bad than by mere rules for hygiene and right living. A conversion is necessary. But this, like freedom itself, requires delicacy of manoeuvre; for moral obsession injects a proprietorial spirit into virtue itself, and obstructs the paths to moral renewal faster than it opens them. The further one's moral anxiety is removed from one's self, the more productive of moral reform it is likely to be: the feeling of impurity, of personal defilement, has its value, but it is still too near to the egocentric fear for one's own integrity, and it can mislead one into dreams or encumber one with scruples. Personal encounter is better: but better still is a sharp and wounding realization of the harm that one has done to others; for the moral 'cogito' develops through suffering alone. The soul that is habituated, either to evil or to good, may be suddenly freed from the vicious circle in which it was contained, by the shock of simply realizing its own weakness.

From that moment, the moral conflict proceeds in two directions. It is necessarily concerned with human discontents and the drama of freedom. An end to these disquietudes would be the end of morality and of all personal life: liberties would be replaced by a legalism which would confirm both social pressures and infantile intimidations; this would eliminate moral initiative and socialize moral criteria, by classifying the righteous and the wicked according to formal regulations. Legalism does not, of course, condemn the law; law remains necessary to any embodied and socialized freedom. Mediating as it does between theory and practice, between the absolute inwardness of moral choice and the propagation of the moral idea to the general public, the law, directed to freedom, is the instrument of our progressive liberation and of our deepening fellowship in a universe of moral persons. But the tension between the ethic of the law and the ethic of love places the vast field of personal morality between the banality of the rule and the paradox of the exception; between the patient trans-formation of everyday life and the wildly reformative efforts of exasperated freedom.[1]

(5) *Art. Sketch for a personalist aesthetic.* The excess of labour in our lives still hides from us the fact that the poetic life constitutes a central aspect of personality, and ought to be reckoned as essential as our daily bread. Transcendent as it is, 'sublime' in the proper sense of the word, art cannot be reduced either to the greed for sensation or the intoxication of life; nor is it, when embodied in its works, reducible to the pure contem-plation of the idea, nor to the constructive power of the mind.

[1] It is in the works of BERDYAEV and in the *Le Devoir* of *Le Senne*, among contemporary writers, that one finds the most profitable reflections upon this subject.

It is the sensitive expression, throughout the whole range of our existence, of life's intimately unexpected character; it delights in disconcerting our customary vision, in shedding a ray of divine light upon a familiar object, or introducing into the realm of the sublime some movingly homely observation. Like the science of wave-mechanics, art brings us into contact with what neither the senses nor the thought can grasp of themselves; it makes us aware of our nearness both to the infernal and the supernal. How distressingly narrow, in this respect, are most of our discussions about realism! It is true enough that many artists of today, in their abstract games, are dissimulating a sense of frustration at the limitations of the human being, whilst others, less exigent, take refuge in cleverness, prettiness or the fashions of the day. It is also true that the dislocated faces and features which some artists make us endure are, from one point of view, symptomatic of the profound nihilism of our epoch. Even so, the crass subservience of other artists to the habitual and the utilitarian is a sign of something graver still, and of less hopeful promise. Realism—yes, but what is reality? The objective world of immediate sensation? But it has now been demonstrated that that world too is permeated throughout with contrivances of the human mind and of social convention. Much so-called 'realism', complacent and commonplace, is merely a compromise, and generally a cheap one, intended to reassure us about reality and not at all to reveal it. Art is, indeed, a protest against this mendacity, in the name of the deeper realities that occasionally flash into our marginal consciousness.

But this indubitably brings us face to face with a problem of communication. Art that appeals only to a small and sophisticated public declines into complexity, enigma and calculation, whereas art needs to be a search for beings and forms which are real. Thus 'realist' by nature, however, art must also be 'abstract', if it be true that the transcendent can communicate itself only indirectly and by signs. As an interpretation of the suprahuman, art cannot wholly avoid obscurity and isolation. It is the most abstract of the physicists, not the cash chemists, who are turning our workaday world upside down; and who knows but that some of the artists who are now the least popular may not rediscover, by one means or another, the way to a great and universally-intelligible art?[1]

(6) *The community of destinies. History.* Is human history, or more explicitly the common destiny of mankind, a value for the world of persons? If persons were no more than free and spontaneous individualities and strictly separate, they would not have *a* history, in the singular, there would be only so many incommunicable histories. History exists because humanity is *one*.

But if the meaning of history could be written in advance, there would be no freedom. And as this is not the case, how can history be effectively studied, when the most learned among us, drawing upon the experience of a wide community, can explore only a small field of history more or less superficially, and not without some distortion of perspective? The worst method is to cram history into a ready-made framework, for then it becomes wholly objective and ceases to be of value; inevitably so, since it can no longer be the object of selection or of love. We also find, in various quarters, presentations of 'the meaning of history' or of its 'providential design', which would render man's own freedom within the collective dialectic undiscoverable—a view that is incompatible with a personal universe. History can only be the co-creation of free men, and whatever its structure or its condition may be, freedom has again to take them in hand. Not that this can be done all at once: there is a margin between the history that is verified and that which is assumed, and that margin is the realm of historical decision. But this refashioning of history is the paramount work of man. It proceeds upon evidence so far con-

[1] *Esprit* Feb. 1947, *Le réel n'est à personne.*

jectural that no one, in the name of History, can forestall events by dictating some hypothesis in advance. Yet under these conditions the common destiny of mankind is quite practically, for any assemblage of persons, one of the supreme values. And with the awakening of the continents and after the devastations of two world wars the lineaments of this destiny begin to appear more clearly than ever before.

(7) *The religious values. Personalism and Christianity.* A Christian personalist has no more to say than any other Christian about Christianity itself. In questions of faith he will only emphasize its personal structure, the limitless though hidden trustfulness and intimacy of the person towards the supreme Person, and the inadequacy, in that relation, of every demonstration or regulation that remains purely objective.[1] But Christianity is also religion, the religion of a transcendence that incarnates itself in a universe and in a body of persons in history. A large part of its actual living is therefore subject to the conditions of nature, time and place, where its creative inspiration is expressed in perishable forms, sometimes in compromises that are suspect. Discrimination between the transcendent inspiration and the ambiguous forms it assumes in its historic context is a labour that has to be incessantly renewed. Whatever is born in time disappears with the passage of time (mediaeval Christendom, for instance, the link between altar and throne). A Christian, mindful of the central importance of the Incarnation in his religion, will not despise these historic realizations because of their impurities, but he will be vigilant to detect any deviations that they introduce into Christian values; and he will seek, not to fix the eternal in such transitory forms, but to make way for its entry into each new phase of history.[2] Finally, Christian personalism will underline,

[1] Concerning the personalist account of the Faith, see J. MOUROUX: *Je crois en toi. Structure personelle de la foi* (Ed. Revue des Jeunes, 1949).

[2] See the study of *Personnalisme et Christianisme* (Esprit, 1940), reprinted in *Liberté sous conditions.*

in opposition to religious individualism, the communal character, too little regarded for the last two centuries, of Christian faith and life. While rediscovering here, in new perspectives, the balance between the subjective and the objective, he will be equally on his guard against religious subjectivism, and against any objectification which tends to impair freedom of action, for this is the source of every authentic religious initiative.

Frustration of value. Suffering. Evil. Negation

The forces working in opposition to values are no less formidable than is the zeal of those who champion them.

Even before it meets with opposition, the urge to achieve value flags from a kind of internal weakness. Enthusiasm becomes clouded-over: knowledge falls short of the complete intelligibility it aims at; art fails to render the miracle of the world altogether present to everyone; morality finds it cannot wholly separate itself from formalism and liberate the human heart; history, that it cannot eliminate violence; religion, that it cannot live by pure spirit. Man's highest mission is dogged by disappointments at every turn, and often cut short by death. Values conflict with one another instead of combining in a harmonious whole. Of a life dedicated to values one may say, as Paul Ricoeur[1] said of the philosophy of Gabriel Marcel, that it alternates between a *lyrical* extreme where value reigns in triumph over a world of progress and ultimate reconciliation, and a *dramatic* extreme where value is everlastingly subject to defeat. Joy is inseparable from the pursuit of values, but no less so is suffering—suffering which is intensified as the progress of culture deepens man's sensitivity to it, and is increased to the extent that personal existence is amplified.

Suffering, it is true, may be richly compensated from the deeper reserves of humanity that it sometimes unlocks. But who can deny the absolute character of evil in certain of its

[1] In his *Gabriel Marcel and Karl Jaspers*. (Edition du Temps présent).

forms? One may try to ascribe it to some impersonal order that depends on the existence of evil (as did Leibnitz, and Malebranche). But this is to juggle away the personal experience we have of it—of its wounding power, as intimate as that of love, of its shocking enormity, and its singular fascination, equal to that of the highest values. Yet if one takes evil for a fatality, what becomes of freedom? In truth, evil begins with personality: without personality the worst there can be is disorder. Evil can take shape only in a conscience, or in a conspiracy of consciences. (For the Christian evil is indeed a Person, as is the Good.) It is the counter-sign of freedom: there could be no real choice in respect of values if freedom did not include liberty to choose dis-values. Nevertheless, as soon as evil appears, it disrupts the personal universe, corrupts and undoes the person. It reminds us that the fulfilment to which the person aspires is not, in our human condition, the fullness of being itself. Our freeedom, emerging from the void, is the spontaneity of negation at the same time as it is the spontaneity of existence. There are extreme circumstances (one remembers some revelations from the world of concentration-camps), and certain border-line experiences such as those of the mystics, in which the horror of nothingness surrounding the pathways to the Absolute is endured to the point of despair, and these provide intimate testimony of the nature of evil.

Is it then being, or the void, is it evil or is it good, that in the end prevails? A kind of joyous assurance, linked with an expansive personal experience, inclines one to the optimistic reply. But neither experience nor reason can answer this question. Those who can, whether Christians or not, do so under the guidance of a faith that reaches beyond all experience.[1]

[1] For example, JASPERS. On the Christian side one may refer, for this aspect of the problem, to *La Petite Peur du XXme siècle* (Ed. du Seuil) and to M. DUBARLE: *Optimisme ou pessimisme* (Ed. Revue des Jeunes).

CHAPTER VII

ENGAGEMENT

THAT existence is action, and that the most perfect existence is the action that is the most perfect, and yet
is still active; this is one of the leading intuitions of
contemporary thought. If some thinkers object to introducing
the notion of action into thought and into the highest spiritual
life, it is because their conception of action is too restricted,
and would limit it to vital impulsion, utility, or becoming.
Here it must be understood in the most comprehensive sense.
Applied to man, it signifies his integral spiritual experience;
applied to being, its interior productivity. One may then say;
whatever is not acting is not. The *logos* is the truth; since
Christianity it is also the way and the life. We are indebted to
Maurice Blondel for having amply substantiated these ideas.

A theory of action therefore is not an appendage to personalism, but is of essential importance in it.

Factors of Frustration

Action presupposes freedom. Teaching that is materialistic
or deterministic, whether implicitly or openly, cannot consis-
tently exhort to action or to the guidance of action. If whatever
happens in the world is regulated in advance by irresistible
processes, what remains for us to do?—except to wait upon
events and regulate our feelings so as to suffer as little as possible, according to the advice of the Stoics and of Spinoza.
Marxism has taken account of this danger, which is involved
in its ambiguous materialism, and is always rallying against

it the resources of the *praxis*. A practically fatalistic conception of the 'meaning of history' or of progress tends simply to justify the conventional conduct of the day. At the present day all parties are suffering from uncertainty about the relations between 'objectivity' and personal responsibility—in other words, between the war and the combatant. Many believe, more or less, that certain trends are 'inevitable' and hope for nothing better than to elude the consequences from day to day, flattering themselves that an attitude of compromise amounts to a position of centrality. Or they put up a show of knowing what must inevitably come to pass, and accoutre themselves in vast ideological systems which, if reality does not proceed accordingly, they want to see imposed by police action. In such a climate of surrender and evasion, it is urgently necessary to restore the sense of responsible personality, and of the authority that the person can wield when it has faith in itself.

It must also be remembered that the person is not isolated. The effort to achieve truth and justice is a collective effort. Not that a million consciences necessarily produce a higher consciousness than does a single strict conscience. Numbers, before they are organised, may only produce mediocrity, confusion, weariness or passion. And at the first attempt, organization often does no more than harden the mass emotions thus brought together. It is only through their personalization that numbers achieve human significance, ensure free co-operation and exchange of gifts, and bring under control the follies and mystifications into which individuals are led through their separation. Research for a 'technique of spiritual procedure'[1] ought not to detach us from the conditions of action and turn us back upon interior purification and moral expression. For in the end no action is valuable unless it be such that the individual conscience, even if in retreat, is growing

[1] See, under this heading, the study published in *Esprit* in November 1934 and February 1935 and the article by ANDRE RIVIER in the issue of October 1938.

in community with the total consciousness and the universal drama of its epoch. And what if one can see no way to make sense, even provisionally, of human nature; what if the universe seems to offer one no value at all? Still, one conclusion valid for action may be drawn—Do what you will, it matters not what, so long as your action is intense and you are vigilant about its consequences.

Some may then decide to create their own values. But their choice of values is arbitrary; and their faithfulness to them, being purely voluntary, is precarious.

Others may take either of two ways. They can refuse to act, concluding that in a world so absurd, there is no sufficient reason for engaging in any one action rather than another. Aesthetic dilettantism, ironic anarchism, a maniacal advocacy of everything non-party, abstentionist, protestant or libertarian, are all prevalent in these quarters. They seldom produce anything more than groups of secessionists, in which proud hearts, meddlesome spirits, fastidious mugwumps and desiccated brains are indistinguishably mingled. An almost visceral repugnance to commit themselves, and an inability to bring anything to realization, betray the dried-up sources of feeling that underlie their sometimes highly-coloured eloquence.

Alternatively, they may be infatuated with the idea that action is now freed from all restraint, and beome fired with a passion for intensity of life. This leads to a kind of frenzy for action; to restless and misconceived agitations among the weaker sort, and among the stronger, to an exaltation of ecstasy or of power. The last is a way strewn with distinguished names, from Ernst von Salomon to Malraux, from Lawrence to Drieu and Junger. But where there is nothing to mark the frontier between the human and inhuman, who is to keep one from inhumanity? Or from yielding to the sub-human in a time of terror?[1]

[1] Upon these questions, see BERTRAND D'ASTORG: *Introduction au monde de la terreur* (Ed. du Seuil), and *Introduction aux existentialismes*, Chap. VI.

The four dimensions of action

What do we expect from action? That it should modify the reality around us, react beneficially upon ourselves, bring us nearer to others, or enrich our world of values? In truth we expect of every action that it should answer all these four purposes more or less, for the whole man in us stoops to drink at every action we perform. There are, nevertheless, types of action of which one or another of these aims is the keynote, the others being only awakened as its harmonics. Let us recall the classical distinctions.

(1) In *making* ($\pi o \epsilon \hat{\iota} v$) the principal aim of the action is to dominate and organize external matter. We will call such action economic; the action of man upon things, and the action of man upon man in the sphere of natural or productive energies, wherever man interferes with, illuminates or makes use of existing causal patterns, even in the material affairs of culture or religion. This is the domain of science in its application to human activities, *of industry* in the widest sense of the word. Its end and its appropriate criterion is *efficiency*. But man has no satisfaction in fabrication and organization unless he finds in them his own dignity, the fraternity of his fellow-workers, and some fulfilment above that of utility: except under these conditions he is not even a good producer, as we know from 'psycho-technic' research. The economist who ignores these conditions is ushering-in the technocrat, who deals with human relations as though they were merely objective laws bearing upon his problems. The economist cannot however definitively resolve his problems except under the guidance of *politics*, which relates them to *ethics*. If the economist hesitates to accept this guidance, it is because he has too often seen sentiment, opinion, partisan intrigue or *à priori* ideology adduced in the name of politics to confuse his calculations; whereas politics is needed to add the rule of ethics to the rigours of technique. It is at the level of politics that an economy becomes personalized and its personnel institutionalised. That is why the

a-political abstentionist, who takes flight from this vital zone of action, whether downwards to the technical or upwards to meditation and character-formation, is in the vast majority of cases a spiritual deserter.

(2) Considered as human behaviour ($\pi\rho\alpha\tau\tau\epsilon\iota\nu$) action is not judged primarily by the accomplishment of an external work but by the edification of the agent, the development of his ability, of his virtues, of his personal integrity. This zone of *ethical action* finds its objective and its criterion in *authenticity*, a note that is strongly emphasized by existentialist thinkers. Here, it matters less what the agent is doing than how he is doing it, and what, by so doing, he is becoming. Not that this ethical consideration is without effect upon an economic order. The Greeks, because they aspired to a kind of measured and contemplative wisdom, which made them think little of power and tended to induce contempt for the material, never elaborated technical civilization, though their leading engineers showed themselves fully capable of it. The suburbs of an individualist society are nothing like a Christian village, nor like a collective city, even though built upon the same site. We have seen that religions give form and character to landscapes and buildings no less, and perhaps more, than do material conditions.

These observations clarify the problem, often so ill-stated, of the end and the means. If it were possible for man to live for a system of purely technical means, the means would be so completely embodied in the end that there would be no possible divergence between the two. In such a system efficiency alone dictates: every means that is effective is good, and is good just because it succeeds. Efficiency governs the way in which problems are stated, and its requirements have to be insistently recalled to anyone who may feel a nostalgia for obstacles, or to any muddlers who, upon the pretext of moralizing action, try to confuse it with their irrelevant intentions.

But upon a basis so purely technical, no relations whatever can be established beween persons. From the moment that a man appears, his presence affects the entire situation. He alters it by the very quality of his presence. Material means themselves become human means, living factors in a human life which they modify, but by which they are modified in their turn, and the person integrates this interaction in the whole process of which it is a part. If the means degrade the human agent, sooner or later they compromise the result. That is why the ethic of a revolutionary movement or of a government is as important, even from the standpoint of ultimate efficiency, as the physical force at its disposal.

Vain is the hope, which technocrats share with the followers of Saint-Simon, that better government could be founded upon the administration of means than upon human relations! Men would soon be treated as if they were mere things in such a world, supposing it were viable. Technics and ethics are the respective modalities of the *operation* and the *presence*, inseparably co-operative, of a being who can act only in proportion to what he is, and can only exist in acting.

(3) θεωρεῖν was the word used by the Greeks for that part of our activity which is engaged in the discernment of values, thereby enriching ourselves and extending the reign of values over all other men. While retaining the classical translation '*contemplative action*', one should observe that this contemplation is not, for us, an operation of the mind alone, but of the whole man; not an evasion of common actions in favour of one that is chosen and isolated, but the aspiration to a realm of values entering into and developing every human activity. Its aim is *perfection* and *universality*, but by way of finite works and particular actions.

Contemplative activity is disinterested, in the sense that it does not aim *directly* at the organization of external relations, either between things or between human beings. It is not disinterested in the sense of remaining indifferent to these relations, without action upon them or sensibility to them. Like every human activity, it takes its first shape from the given conditions. The organization of monastic studies is feudal with the Benedictines, collegiate with the Dominicans, military with the Jesuits, according to the needs of their respective times. But such activity influences, in its turn, the entire field of practical activity—and this in two ways.

First, indirectly, through the diversion of a superabundant activity. It is the highest mathematical speculations, the least directly useful, which have found the most fruitful applications, and at the same time the most unforeseen—the application of astronomical calculations to navigation, for instance, and the discovery of atomic energy as a by-product of lay research into the structure of matter. The two centuries of theological controversy which established the full significance of the Incarnation of Christ also founded the only fully activist and industrial civilizations. We may even speak here of *contemplative induction*. These experiences should restrain us from condemning any activity, simply because it is of no immediately visible use, as useless *à priori*.

The contemplative, while maintaining as his dominant interest the exploration and realization of values, may also aim directly at the disruption of existing practice. His action is then of the type that we call *prophetic*. Prophetic action maintains a relation between the contemplative and the practical, as political action does between ethics and economics. For example, it may affirm the absolute in all its trenchancy, by speech, writing or behaviour, when its meaning has been blunted by compromises. Of this type of action are Pascal's *Lettres Provinciales*, and Zola's *J'accuse*, also the obedience of Abraham, the protest of the conscientious objector, the hunger-strikes of Gandhi. One could even speak of *prophetic institutions*, which have significance inasmuch as they bear witness of a world to come. But they lose it when they present themselves as cells of an organization that would contract out of the world (phalanges, Boismendau communities etc.) The prophetic gesture may be one of 'desperation' (practically speaking), sure of immediate defeat, obeying only an irresistible call to bear witness to an absolute with absolute disinterestedness. But to suppose that it is invariably desperate and can have no aim beyond a sort of forlorn affirmation is to confound the species with the genus. To make a virtue of failure and futility, to forsake the modesties of real responsibility for who knows what obscure aspirations towards martyrdom—this is more often a sign of devitalization than of spirituality. The prophetic gesture can be formed with conscious will to have an effect upon the situation, although by means that derive more from faith in the transcendent power of the absolute than in any efficient causes it may set in motion. The prophet may even grasp the situation in all its depths so fully that his witness turns into a practical action: Joan of Arc, who began as a simple witness to her 'voices' went on to take command of an army. However, if the prophet thinks no scorn of efficiency—differing in that from the spiritual 'emigrant'—he never *schemes* for it like a politician; he presses forward in the invincible power of his faith; in the assurance that if he achieves no immediate end he will at least succeed in sustaining the vital awareness of men at the elevation from which alone it can break into history.

(4) We need not again consider the collective dimension of action. To its complete humanization, the community of labour, a common destiny or spiritual community are indispensable. It is by offering these things, or some mixture of them, to those who could not find them in the environment of their lives or in their countries, that fascism and communism owe a great deal of their fascination. The clamours of solitary desperadoes will never again, in our age, awaken men to action that is a redemption from despair.

ENGAGEMENT

The political and the prophetic poles. The theory of self-commitment

Such is the total range of action. It is not enough, as we know, to affirm the unity of theory and practice in a general way. We have to map out the entire geography of action, to know all that needs to be unified, and how. No action will be healthy or effectual which altogether neglects, or still worse rejects, either the need for efficiency or the influence of the spiritual life. Clearly, the inability of each man fully to realize everyman, imposes the need for specialized action. Technician, politician, moralist, prophet and contemplative frequently irritate one another. No one can be everything at once. But action, in the current meaning of the term, that which takes effect upon public life, cannot without disequilibrium be founded upon anything narrower than the whole field that stretches from the political pole to the prophetic pole. The accomplished man of action has in himself this double polarity and is able to manoeuvre between the one and the other, striving by turns to ensure the autonomy and regulate the power of each, and to find ways of communication between them. The political temperament which lives by arrangements and compromises, and the prophetic temperament which lives by meditation and spiritual valour, cannot as a rule co-exist in the same person. For great concerted actions it is indispensable that we bring men of both kinds into reciprocal and complementary action: otherwise the prophets in their isolation will turn to vain imprecation, while the tacticians become entangled in their own manoeuvres. Let us consider these two requirements a little more closely.

A philosophy for which absolute values exist is tempted to put off action until the cause is perfect and the means irreproachable. But this amounts to renunciation of action. The Absolute is not of this world nor even commensurable with it. We are never actually engaged except in questionable conflicts for causes more or less impure;[1] and to refuse to engage in them for that reason is a refusal to accept the human condition. We aspire to purity: but too often what is called purity is the exposition of a general idea, an abstract principle, of an imaginary situation or of noble sentiments set forth with an intemperate taste for capital letters—the very reverse of personal heroism. Fussy counsels of perfection commonly go with a lofty narcissism egocentrically preoccupied with an individual integrity cut off from the collective drama, or, at the extreme of banality, they may dress-up pusillanimity, indeed even puerility, in a mantle of regal impotence.[2] Here the sense of the absolute loses itself in dubious psychic complications. But not only are we never confronted with an ideal situation; we can seldom choose the critical moments at which our intervention is required. They challenge us in forms unforeseen by our philosophy—and suddenly. We have to respond impromptu, to hazard an opinion or invent a new one, just when our laziness was getting ready to study the matter. People always speak of 'engagement', as if it depended upon ourselves: but we *are engaged*, embarked, already involved. Abstention is only a delusion. Scepticism also is a philosophy; the notion of non-intervention, between 1936 and 1939, brought about the war with Hitler; for whoever will 'have nothing to do with politics' passively furthers the politics of the *de facto* power.

Nevertheless, though to 'engage' oneself is to consent to make-shift, to something impure ('dirtying one's hands'), and to accept one's limitations, it does not sanctify one's abdication

[1] See *Esprit*, special number: *Notre action* Oct. 1938, notably P. L. LANDSBERG: *Le Sens de l'action* (in that number) and *Réflexions sur l'engagement personnel* (*Esprit* Nov. 1937). This theme of 'engagement' which moreover goes back to Scheler and Jaspers, was introduced into France by *Esprit* before 1939 before it was taken up by existentialism in 1945 and soon exploited to the point of abuse. Cf. also D'ASTORG *Introduction aux existentialismes*, Chap. IV.

[2] On this theme, see *Qu'est-ce que le personnalisme?* (Ed. du Seuil), Chap. I.

of personality or any abandonment of the values that it serves. The creative force of self-commitment is born of the tension that it excites between the imperfection of the cause and its own absolute fidelity to the values implicated. The troubled and sometimes agonized conscience caused by the impurities of our cause should keep us far from fanaticism, in a state of vigilant criticism. In sacrificing views and harmonies that we have imagined, to the demands of reality we acquire a kind of virility, that which comes from being stripped of naïveties and illusions, and from having continually to strive for fidelity in disconcerting circumstances. The risks we have to run, and the partial obscurity in which we have to take decisions, put us in the state of dispossession, insecurity and hardihood which is the climate of all great action.

When once that tragic atmosphere of action has been experienced, it is no longer possible to confuse *engagement* with *regimentation*. We learn that the cause of the good and the cause of evil can rarely be contrasted simply as white and black, that sometimes there is but a hair's breadth between the cause of truth and the cause of error. We no longer dread to recognize, and openly to fight, the weaknesses on our own side; we see the relativity of all action, the persistent peril of collective blindness, the menace in systems and dogmatisms. We refuse to substitute for the dilettantism of abstention a dilettantism of adherence, or to mistake for virile action those careers of disaster, embraced in the name of some conformity, which are the opposite of adult behaviour—puerile suicides that cut short some infantile ambition. But we also realize that action is a way of knowing, and that to recognize and take that way may be to win the truth, be it only by a hair's breadth.

Action in this sense is not easy. Fanatics scorn it as hesitant, because it refuses to idolize anything relative and respects vigilance. Politicians reproach it as intractable because it never forgets claims that are absolute. But courage lies in acceptance of these inconvenient conditions, in refusal to forsake them for

H

the velvet sward of eclecticism, idealism or opportunism. Integral action is always dialectical. Often it has to keep hold, in obscurity and doubt, of the two ends of a chain that it knows not how to rivet, or—for a more active metaphor—of two levers of a machine whose action it cannot harmonize. It must press first one and then the other, trying first tactics and then prophetic witness, engagement and then disengagement, mediation and then rupture of relations; not in an arbitrary alternation of which each movement annuls the one before it, but like an engineer with a machine that is out of order, making each adjustment the means to the next, and every time getting it more nearly into working order.

The education that is provided in these days is almost the worst possible preparation for such a culture. The universities distribute formal knowledge which predisposes men to ideological dogmatism or, by reaction, to sterile irony. The spiritual educators, too often, base moral edification upon scrupulousness and moral casuistry instead of the cultivation of decision. The whole climate of education needs to be changed if we no longer want to see, on the plane of action, intellectuals who set an example of blindness and men of conscience who inculcate cowardice.

PART TWO

PERSONALISM AND THE REVOLUTION OF THE TWENTIETH CENTURY

PART TWO

PERSONALISM AND THE REVOLUTION OF THE TWENTIETH CENTURY

PERSONALISM AND THE REVOLUTION
OF THE TWENTIETH CENTURY

THOUGHT and action being so inseparably united in personalist doctrine, the reader will expect some definition of action not only in general method and perspective, but in some precise lines of conduct. A personalism that was content with speculation about the structure of the personal universe would belie its name.

However, the links between ends and means are not immediate or obvious, on account of the complexity introduced into their relations by the transcendence of values. Two men who were in agreement with all that is in the preceding pages might disagree about the problems of the state schools in France, or which trade union they would prefer, or what economic associations ought to be encouraged. There is nothing unusual in that: Sorel was an inspiration to both Lenin and Mussolini. Action is thought-out by reflection upon certain concrete analyses and practical alternatives, viewed in the light of a spectrum of values. Values may be held in common while the analyses differ and expectations diverge. Even such a philosophy as Marxism, wholly subordinated to politico-social analysis, can guarantee no direct deductions from its analyses to its precepts: unless we are mistaken, both Trotsky and Léon Blum thought themselves as good Marxists as Stalin.

Since the 1930's, personalist principles have been applied to a certain historic situation, in a phase of militant thinking. We would not identify personalism in detail with these applications of it, which do not pretend to be exhaustive or definitive;

97

but they are at least illustrative, and give outline to a movement which is not without unity. Let us examine them.

The European Nihilism

This reaction began in the crisis of 1929, which sounded the knell of Europe's happiness and directed attention to revolutions already under way. Of the troubles and miseries which ensued, some gave purely technical and others purely moral explanations. A few young men thought that the disease was at the same time economic and moral, both in the social structure and in the hearts of men; that no remedy was possible without both an economic and a spiritual revolution; and that, man having become what he is, we should have to find and loosen the knots that bind him in the one respect and in the other. First we had to analyse both crises in order to clear the way.

The spiritual crisis is that of classical European man, born into the bourgeois world. He had believed that he was realizing the ideal of the reasonable animal, that triumphant reason was successfully domesticating the animal in him whilst well-being neutralized its passions. Three shocks of warning were administered within a century to this civilization over-confident of its stability. Marx revealed, underneath its economic progress, the merciless struggle of profound social forces; Freud exposed, beneath its psychological complacencies, the witches' cauldron of rebellious instincts; Nietzsche, finally, proclaimed the nihilism of Europe before yielding the floor to Dostoievsky. Since then, their themes have been richly orchestrated by two world wars, the arrival of police states and an underworld of concentration camps. Today, European nihilism is spreading and organizing its forces in every field left vacant by the retreat of those substantial beliefs which kept our fathers in heart— the Christian faith, the culture of science, of reason and of duty. This desperate world has its philosophers, whose teaching is of absurdity and despair, its authors who sow mockery to the four winds. It has its masses, who are less destructive. 'The supreme despair,' wrote Kierkegaard, 'is not to feel desperate.' The reign of satisfied mediocrity is, without doubt, the contemporary basis of nihilism and, as Bernanos has it, of the demoniac.

One can no longer tell what man is, and as we watch him today undergoing such astonishing transformations, some think there is no such thing as human nature. For some people, this idea becomes translated into 'everything is *possible* for man', and in that they find some hope; for others, 'everything is *permissible* to man', and with that they abandon all restraint; for others, finally, 'everything is *permissible against* man', and with that we have arrived at Buchenwald. All the games that might divert us from our disarray have lost their savour, or have been indulged in to satiety. The play of ideas has yielded all it has to give in Hegel—he marks, in fact, the end of philosophy, inasmuch as philosophy is a scholarly architecture designed to conceal our suffering. The religious lunacy which worships the God of philosophers and bankers would indeed justify us in proclaiming that God is dead, if that idol were he. Could we have only a little respite from the wars, to carry on with our technical miracles, then, glutted with comfort, we should soon be able to declare that happiness was dead. Another fourteenth century, as it were, is crumbling away before our eyes: the time for 'a second Renaissance' is at hand.[1]

A crisis in social organization is involved with this spiritual collapse. In the midst of a distracted economy, science continues serenely on its course, redistributing riches and altering social pressures, until social classes fall apart, and the most responsible classes sink into incompetence and indecision. The State has to collect its forces in this tumult: and in the end war or the preparation for war, which is the end-result of such ubiquitous conflict, has for thirty years paralysed both our progress to-

[1] This was the theme of the leading article, *Refaire la Renaissance*, in the first number of Esprit in 1932.

wards the betterment of living conditions and the higher functions of our collective existence.

The rejection of nihilism

Three attitudes towards this total crisis are much in evidence.

Some people give way to fear, and its most usual symptom is the conservative appeal to pre-existing ideas and established powers. The stratagem of the conservative mind is to exalt the past as a pseudo-tradition, or even as pseudo-nature, and to condemn everything modern by the authority of this formal abstraction. It is a defence by prestige; nevertheless it compromises, by withdrawing them from life, the very values it purports to be saving. It is a move for security which exposes its flanks to vengeance and destruction.

Others seek refuge in the cult of catastrophe. They sound the apocalyptic trumpet, minimising every progressive effort with the argument that eschatology alone is worthy of noble souls: they inveigh against all the disorders of the times, or at least against all those that confirm their prejudices. This is a neurosis that is typical of periods of crisis, the inspiration of mystagogues innumerable.

There is one way out, and only one—that is, to confront the event, to invent, and to go ahead—the way which, since the dawn of life, has alone enabled life to cope with crises. The creatures whose effort to surmount danger were limited to withdrawals into sheltered quarters are those that burdened themselves with shell or carapace: they became mussels or oysters, the waifs and strays of life. It was the fish, who took the risk of a naked skin and the hazards of travel, whose initiative led at last to *homo sapiens*. But this affirmative line may be taken in different ways.

We do not disparage the conservative myth of stability in order to commend a myth of blind adventurousness. This, in the face of mediocrity, boredom and despair, has been the temptation of many young men, and of some of the best, in the earlier years of the twentieth century. Lawrence, Malraux and Jünger were among their teachers, as Nietzsche was their foundation. 'A man who is active and at the same time pessimistic' said Manuel in his *l'Espoir*, 'has the makings of a fascist in him, unless he has some fidelity behind him.' For in his solitariness overshadowed by death, what else is there to do, but to plunge into the intoxication of some vivid, unique career, defying all obstacles, rules and regulations; to seek in emotional paroxysms some substitute for a living faith, hoping to leave somewhere upon this accursed world at least a lasting scar? That way, at whatever cost in cruelty, he thinks to regain the sense that he exists, a feeling which frenzy itself no longer gives him. Existentialism has a certain bias in the same direction, but the swindling and brigandage of the years of war are at least equally responsible for mixing this cocktail of theatrical realism. Alcohol to drown all problems, but only for him who knows the way to get it—we have now seen how this ends, in collective crime.[1]

Is it to avoid this fate, that so many others give themselves up body and soul to the instructions of a party? Rather suddenly, it has become the fashion to praise conformity. In so far as this shows a new sense of the collective task, tinged with a nostalgia for the churches of long ago, there is a certain modesty, a regard for community and sacrifice about it—something certainly more respectable than the intellectual anarchism that either ends at thirty years of age in a solicitor's office or goes on for ever from one café table to another. But of what use is it, without the spirit of freedom and the spirit of truth?

From all these observations one can, it would seem, deduce a few rules of personalist strategy.

(1) At least in the beginning, independence of established

---

[1] These *pseudo-spiritual fascist values* were denounced in a special number of *Esprit* (September 1933), also in December 1947 (*La Pause des fascismes est terminée*) and, in less political context, they figured in an *Interrogation à Malraux* (October 1948).

groups and parties is required, in order to find one's bearings. This does not connote any anarchism or rejection of politics in principle: indeed, wherever individual membership of a collective activity leaves one sufficient freedom of action, it is to be preferred to isolation.

(2) Although spirit is no wild or magical force, there is always a risk of mystification in the affirmation of spiritual values alone, unaccompanied by any precise statement of means and conditions for acting upon them.

(3) The solidarity of the 'spiritual' and the 'material' implies that, in every question, all its problematic aspects must be envisaged, ranging from the 'vilest' data to the 'noblest', with equal accuracy from the one pole to the other. Confusion of mind is the greatest enemy to comprehensive thinking.

(4) Regard for freedom and regard for reality alike demand that the required research should be on its guard against all *à priori* dogmatism, and be ready for anything, even for a change in its whole direction, in order to keep faith with reality and with its own spirit.

(5) The immense accumulation of disorders in our world has led some personalists to call themselves revolutionaries. Facile employment of this word too often renders it devoid of meaning. A sense of the great continuities of life forbids our acceptance of the *tabula rasa* myth of revolution: a real revolution is always a morbid crisis, and it never achieves any automatic solution. To be revolutionary means no more, and also no less, than that the disorders of this century are too intimate and obstinate to be eliminated without reversing the engines, without a profound revision of values, a reorganization of systems and a replacement of those who occupy the most socially responsible places. This having been said, there is no greater abuse of the word than to label yet another conformity with it, or to employ it as a trump in argument or as a substitute for thinking.

Economic society

Marxism is right in giving a certain primacy to economics. Few people despise economics, except those who have ceased to be harassed by any nervousness about their daily bread; and in order to convert the latter, a tour of slumland is preferable to any arguments. At the elementary stage of history which we have thus far attained, economic needs and habits, interests and frustrations do determine the behaviour and the opinions of men in the mass. But this does not mean that economic values are the only ones, or that they are superior to others: the primacy of economics marks a historic disorder from which we have to extricate ourselves.

To find the way out, it is not enough to persuade men, we have also to master material things. Economic disorder can only be cured with economic means, if not by those means alone.

Upon the technical aspects of this disorder, personalism as such has nothing to say; it can only study and draw conclusions like anyone else. It concludes, broadly speaking, that capitalism in Europe, in all its diverse forms, is exhausted and at the end of its devices. American capitalism, still in its phase of expansion, can keep that of Europe alive a little longer by affording it transfusions of credit, but sooner or later, living as it does upon the same principles, it will encounter equally serious contradictions. This development needs however to be closely and critically watched; we must not apply the same stereotyped notion of 'capitalism' to every form it may take, regardless of what is in fact happening.

Such critical observation, brought into the personalist perspective, will coincide with Marxist analysis at several points. Liberal democracy has enabled man to become, politically, a subject, but for the most part he remains an object on the plane of economic existence. The anonymous power of money,[1] by which he is privileged to participate in the

---

[1] *Esprit* October 1933 *L'argent, misère du pauvre, misère du riche.*

profits and advantages this kind of world affords, hardens class distinctions and alienates the real man from them. He needs to recover his own disposition; his values, which the tyranny of production for profit has subverted; his sanity, unhinged by the follies of speculation. If he does not, financial imperialism, wherever it feels itself menaced, will not scruple to turn against the liberties it defended while they were useful to it, and will entrust its ultimate security to reigns of terror or to inexpiable wars.

Capitalism cannot be replaced by some new, fully-fledged régime: economic evolution is too continuous for that. It is within the full-grown body of capitalism itself that the embryonic forms of the socialist world first appear and it is these forms that we have to extend and develop, if by socialism we mean the following:—The abolition of the proletarian condition; the supersession of the anarchic economy of profit by an economy directed to the fulfilment of the totality of personal needs; the socialization, without state monopoly, of those sectors of industry which otherwise foster economic chaos;[1] the development of co-operative life;[2] the rehabilitation of labour;[3] the promotion, in rejection of all paternalist compromises, of the worker to full personality;[4] the priority of labour over capital; the abolition of class distinctions founded upon the division of labour or of wealth; the priority of personal responsibility over the anonymous organization.

From the adoption of socialism as the general directive idea for social reorganization, it does not follow that one must approve every measure that may be proposed in its name.

[1] Concerning nationalization, see *Esprit* April 1945 and January 1946, and concerning property, the special number *De la propriété capitaliste à la propriété humaine.* April 1934

[2] See treatment of *syndicalism* in special numbers of *Esprit* July 1936, March 1937.

[3] Special number of *Esprit* on *Le Travail et l'homme* July 1933

[4] *Esprit*, special number of March 1936: *La personne ouvrière.*

Sometimes socialism goes to sleep, and sometimes it loses its way, or becomes perverted under bureaucratic or police systems. All the greater is the need for a re-edition of socialism, rigorous and at the same time democratic. That is the invention now required of Europe, towards which personalism seeks to contribute in its own way. The future will determine whether personalists ought to work in other ways, according to the lessons of experience.

From this point of view, human problems and the problems of social organization are indivisible: the great question of the twentieth century, without doubt, will be whether it can avoid that dictation by the technocrats, either from the right or the left, which loses sight of man in the organizing of his activities. But to keep the two series of problems in practical relation is far from easy. Certain thinkers are tempted to construct an economy *à priori* in the image of man, rather like the first builders of the motor-car, who encumbered the development of its proper structure by designing it in the form of the horse-drawn carriage. Some of these imagine a corporative economy[1] modelled upon the human organism, and postulate a harmony of workers, employers, nation and state by a mythical analogy which is in striking contradiction with the actual and enduring divergences of interests. Others, who pay attention to inter-personal relations, imagine a society in which economic relations would be man-to-man relations indefinitely multiplied into galaxies of little groups 'upon the human scale', as in the myth of Proudhon. But modern economy is a given reality, which seems to evolve rather like physics, towards the concrete by means of the abstract. It is the abstract equations of aerodynamics that have given the aeroplane its form, supple and beautiful as that of a bird; and no doubt it will be from formulas, at first far removed from the principles of corporative or contractual economics, that we shall evolve the simple but unforeseeable structures of a truly human economy.

[1] *Esprit*, September 1934, special number; *Duplicités du corporatisme.*

There remains the question of means: how do we go from the present economic disorders to the order of tomorrow? The means will doubtless vary with circumstances. The extension of capitalism over the whole globe and its possible unification under one powerful empire render it improbable that this transition can be made without resistances and crises. Parliamentary democracy, which has shown itself incapable of effecting profound economic reforms upon the national scale, can hardly be expected to do so in a far vaster sphere. A 'labour policy without Labour', springing simply from the conciliatory good-will of the enlightened section of the middle classes, has demonstrated its impotence throughout the European resistance movements. The attainment of socialism must be, as it was originally formulated, a work of the workers themselves, of movements of peasants and workers organized with the more enlightened portions of the bourgeoisie. Whether it will be achieved piecemeal or in one piece, quickly or slowly, directly or in roundabout ways, are secrets of the future. But its visage will be that which these movements will have impressed upon it: hence the importance of vigilance, not only with regard to the success of these movements but to their integrity.

Family and society. The relations of the sexes

To human affairs no exclusive categories apply. The family, which attains the status of a society in its biological aspect, is also in other aspects one of the most spiritual social forms. Its narrownesses and its evils have been denounced to satiety by modern writers, whilst others have extolled it only this side idolatry and cried sacrilege upon all who drew attention to its limitations. In truth it deserves neither such excess of praise nor such derogation.

It is primarily a biological structure, complicated, seldom wholly healthy, which gives rise to innumerable individual and collective dramas by its internal emotional disequilibria.

Its carnal character, even when it is healthy, frequently obscures its spirituality; but on the other hand, also endows it with the substance and the intimate illumination which are its essential poesy.

It is a social cell, the first society known to the child, where it learns what human relations are: the family develops these relations as far as the heart is capable of them, and that is its grandeur: but also its weakness, for its members are often deprived of that degree of mutual distance which is necessary for intimacy itself; their spiritual vitality is menaced by the wear and tear of constant contact and by the passions of the tribe. In the end, its internal tensions communicate themselves to the society of which it is a cell: plenty of political and religious rebellions are revolts that were repressed in the familial past. The liabilities in which the family involves us are indeed too heavy to permit any excessive idealization. They make some people unable to see it as anything but a reactionary force.[1]

Yet the family is not only biologically or socially useful, and many of those who defend it simply in its functional aspect miss its full significance. It is the place of contact between public and private affairs, combining a certain range of social relations with a certain intimacy. It socialises the private life while it interiorises the life of manners and customs. Through this mediatory function, the family becomes an essential factor in the personal universe. When it sinks down under the weight of the flesh, it devitalises those whom it was its duty to lead beyond itself, towards higher forms of society. And when it tries completely to socialize itself, infatuated with a kind of family imperialism, there are few more unseemly spectacles. The family with its hackles up, angrily asserting proprietary rights over all its members—whoever delights to see the family in this repulsive light has never understood anything

---

[1] Against which the little book by JEAN LACROIX is a reaction: *Force et faiblesse de la famille* (Ed. du Seuil, 1948), largely in agreement with a rather earlier book by L. DOUCY.

of its miraculous but fragile fabric, woven by love, in which it is the greatest educator. On the other hand, the family can be stifled when it is confused with a stuffy intimacy, shutting-out every draught of fresh air. The charms of private life are the opium of the bourgeoisie, or its hiding-hole from the misery of the world. The values of privacy need rescuing from that profanation.

The family, a biological community, undergoes modifications of structure imposed by its environmental conditions which can profoundly alter its expression without touching its real being. The organization of youth, as an independent age-group,[1] the increase of mobility and of removals, and the democratization of manners are slowly taking the old structure of the family to pieces. If it is true that the increasing laxity of morals and the expiring antics of individualism are dangerously undermining the family as an institution, and spoiling some of its greatest values, we must not confuse such decomposition with its needed ventilation, or with its promotion to a more universal status.

In the perspective we have just outlined, we should be able rightly to place the problems of the sexual life, upon which the great philosophies themselves are so peculiarly discreet. Sexual problems cannot be reduced, as a certain kind of family idealism gives us to understand, to the problems of the family itself; closely though they concern that interior order which the family manifests upon the social plane. Man and woman can only find fulfilment in one another, and their union only finds its fulfilment in the child; such is their inherent orientation towards a kind of abundance and overflow, not to an intrinsic and utilitarian end. Sexual isolation, and child-lessness in marriage, engender a whole series of problems, which in part are of potential value and in part merely produced by the unnatural privation. To conceal these is to main-

1 *Esprit*, special number: *Mouvements et Institutions de jeunesse*, October, 1945.

tain, and often to provoke, the disorders that they are accused of fostering. But they can only be clearly understood when the particular conditions of privation are viewed in relation to the human condition as a whole.

It is too naïve to indict bourgeois respectability for having invented sexual pharisaism, of which it has, however, developed some peculiarly odious forms both from fear and self-interest. Morality would be better served by a little more honesty and a less sordid view of sex.

This is no less true of the vast question of the position of women, in which pseudo-'mystery' we are still far from having disentangled the permanent from the merely historical. Neither masculine self-sufficiency nor the exasperation of vengeful feminism will ever elucidate this dilemma. It is nevertheless true that our social world is one that man has made for men, and that the resources of feminine being are among those which humanity still largely neglects. How these resources are to be fully developed and drawn upon without imprisoning woman in her functions; how to unite her with the world and the world with her; what new values and what new conditions this project calls for—these are questions and tasks inescapable for everyone who gives its full meaning to the affirmation that woman, also, is a person.[1]

National and international society

The nation represents an element of mediation more universalising in its effects than the family. It educates and develops the rational man, enriches the social man by the complexity of the environment it offers him, and opens out before him the entire range of his possibilities. Its correlative danger lies in its greater generality, which renders it so little resistant to the appeals of impassioned verbalism, under the tutelage of vested interests or of the state. Nationalism today appears,

[1] See the special number of *Esprit*, June 1936; *La Femme aussi est une personne.*

in many respects, superannuated, ruinous and regressive. Nevertheless, the national sense is still a powerful corrective of the vital egoism of individuals and of families, of the domination of the state, and of servility towards cosmopolitan economic interests. Human equilibrium is in part regulated from this higher level, which concerns not only citizenship; the nation is one of the integrating factors in man's spiritual life. It may be destined one day to disappear, but its mediating role is still indispensable.

The nation becomes introverted, and a seed-bed of war, if it is not built into a community of nations. The mistake made by the best minds after 1918, was to believe, on liberal, ideological grounds, that this international community could be built simply upon the foundations of sentiment, juridical agreements and parliamentary institutions; whilst other passional, economic and social forces were arousing conflicts and leading to explosions. This illusion persists in the second after-war period (in the U.N.O.) with a more cynical attitude to force: thus evil is piled upon evil. Nevertheless, the world is in fact becoming more and more international: there are no more 'independent' nations in the old sense of the word. The prevailing winds are all making towards world unity, and will sooner or later bring it about, if three conditions can be fulfilled:—namely, that the nations give up their complete sovereignty, not for the benefit of some super-imperialism but to a democratic community of peoples; that this union be achieved between the peoples and their representatives, not between the several governments; and that the forces making for imperialism, especially the economic forces which act sometimes in national and sometimes in cosmopolitan disguise, can be kept under control by the united peoples. Until then, every international organization will be undermined from within by movements that tend to war. Federalism, as a utopian directive, is indeed an expression of personalism:[1] but a directive utopia, whether its character be pacifist[2] or federalist,[3] ought never to be allowed to become an actual utopia, thereby hiding from itself the direction imposed upon it by circumstances, sometimes against its will.

In this epoch particular mention must be made of inter-racial society. The doctrine of the equality of persons obviously excludes every form of racialism, and of xenophobia: which is not in the least to say that it denies the gravity of the practical problems presented by ethnic differences. The colonial period is nearing its end, and justice requires that the metropolitan societies should effectively and loyally pilot towards independence those peoples whose education they have undertaken, and whom they have in some cases uprooted from a social equilibrium quite as valuable as their own. The slightest degree of clairvoyance should warn them not to throw back into chaos those peoples, by whose aid alone are they likely to be able to salvage and continue their own past achievements in new communities of nations.[4]

The State. Democracy. Sketch of a personalist doctrine of power

Politics is not an end in itself, over-ruling all other aims. Nevertheless, if politics is not everything, it enters into everything.

[1] This is a thesis that was advanced by *Esprit: L'Europe contre les hégémonies,* in November 1938, and it is sustained today in European councils (though not always with the above reservations) by publicists of such personalist tendency as Alexandre Marc, Henri Brugmans and Denis de Rougemont.

[2] See special number of *Esprit,* February 1949, *Révision des pacifismes.*

[3] See special number of *Esprit,* November 1948: *Les deux visages du fédéralisme Européen.*

[4] Upon the Jewish question, see *Esprit,* May 1933, Sept. 1945, Oct. 1947. Upon the colonial question, *Dossiers d'Indochine,* Dec. 1933, A.E.F. two educational numbers; *Le Colonialisme, son avenir, sa liquidation:* Dec. 1935, and *Dernières Chances de l'Union Française,* July 1949. Upon xenophobia and the problems of aliens, the number on *L'Emigration, problème revolutionnaire,* July 1931.

The first point of reference here should be the rightful place of the State. The State, let us repeat, is not the nation, nor even a condition that must be fulfilled before the nation can attain to veritable being.[1] Only fascists openly proclaim their aim to be the good of the State. The State is that which gives objectivity, strength and concentration, to human rights; it emerges spontaneously from the life of organized groups (G. Gurvitch), and in this respect it is the institutional guarantee of the person. The State is meant for man, not man for the State.

The crucial problem for personalism is that of the legitimacy of power wielded by man over man, which seems to be incompatible with the interpersonal relation: the anarchists indeed think it is so.[2] They believe that the affirmation of the individual, free of all constraint, would spontaneously and of itself bring about a collective order; and that power, on the other hand, is inevitably corrupt and oppressive, however it be constituted. The liberal thesis is not essentially different from this. At the very opposite extreme we have the theorists of absolute power, who think that man, being incurably egoistic, is incapable of raising himself to the level of a common law, and must be forcibly constrained to observe it. On the one side, then, we see optimism about the person but pessimism about power, and on the other pessimism about the person but optimism about power. In both these views of the relation between the personal and the collective one term is idealised and the other degraded. Anarchism and liberalism forget that since man's personality is deeply rooted in the natural world it is impossible to exercise power over things without exercising

[1] E. MOUNIER: *Anarchie et personnalisme* (*Esprit*, April 1937). Upon the problem of the State, consult the works of G. GURVITCH, and at the same time see J. LACROIX: *Personne et amour*; DE ROUGEMONT *Politique de la personne* (Albin Michel).

[2] So did Marx himself, who prophesied that in the future the State would wither away.

some constraint over men. However, if this necessity makes power inevitable, it does not endow it with authority. Authority can be founded only upon the final destiny of the person, which power ought to respect and promote. Several things follow from this:—

In the first place, that the person ought to be protected against abuses of power, and that all power not subject to a higher power tends to corrupt. The pre-requisites for this protection are—public and statutory recognition of the person[1] and constitutional limitation of the powers of the State; a balance between the central and the local authorities; the established right of appeal by the citizen against the State; *habeas corpus;* limitation of the powers of the police, and the independence of the judicial authority.

Where the person has to be subordinate, it is the more essential to safeguard his sovereignty as a subject, and to reduce to the minimum such irresponsibility as the very condition of being governed imposes upon him. This is the real problem of *democracy*, a word surrounded with ambiguities. Sometimes it is the name of a form of government, at other times it is used for spontaneous arbitrament by the masses, but it is, in intention, the research for a form of government erected upon the spontaneity of the masses in order to ensure their participation as subjects in the objective structure of powers. Though the two things cannot be separated, they need to be distinguished: for either the 'mob-rule' at the one extreme or the irremovable one-party State at the other are but different kinds of irresponsible tyranny.

The sovereignty of the public cannot be based on the authority of numbers; the dictate of the many—or of the majority—is just as arbitrary as one person's good pleasure. Nor, as Rousseau rightly perceived, can authority be turned

[1] This, proposed by *Esprit* in 1939, was followed up in the same review in 1944-5, by a project for a declaration which had some influence upon the new French Constitution of 1946.

I*

over to an anarchic sovereignty of free individuals; it is the attribute of a society rationally organized in a juridical order; the basis of authentic sovereignty lies in human rights. Rights, which constitute the middle term between freedom and organization, maintain the sphere of action in which it is possible for the collective drama to proceed, between individual liberties and the progressive personalization of powers. And here popular initiative is effective in two ways—

Indirectly through representatives, as sincere, public-spirited and able as are obtainable, of the citizens' will.[1] This presupposes a preponderant concern with political education, a function for which political parties have long had the responsibility. When they become mere 'electoral machinery' for de-personalizing both reformers and electors by administrative delays, internal conformity and ideological petrifaction, these parties are dismissing themselves from their business. Unable to get beyond the liberal stage of democracy, diffident about their ideology, their tactics and the social classes for which they must still act, willy-nilly, as rubber-stamps, they will surely soon be superseded. Reform of the party system might palliate these evils, but could not now cure them. Only on the foundation of a new social structure will democracy be able to build up, not a single-party totalitarian system that would perpetuate and intensify its existing defects, but new systems of education and political procedure corresponding to the altered conditions of society.[2] If representation is to be sincere it must also be incorruptible by the temptations of power. It presupposes that the political life is spontaneous as well as unrepressed; that the majority will govern always for the good of all citizens and their education, and will not seek the suppression of the minority.

The sovereignty of the people still finds expression, when

---

[1] *Le Problème de la représentation,* special number of *Esprit,* Mar. 1939
[2] *Le Régime des partis, Bilan-avenir,* special number of *Esprit,* May 1939
Le Problème du statut des partis, by FRANCOIS GOGUEL *Esprit,* Jan. 1946

its representatives fail in their function, in direct pressure upon the government—in meetings of protest, disturbances, seditious groups and associations, strikes, boycotts and, in the extreme case, in national insurrection. The State, itself born in strife but forgetful of its origins, usually regards such acts of pressure as illegal; they are nevertheless profoundly legitimate if a State is condoning injustice or oppression. We must never forget that during the century and a half that has elapsed since the beginning of the labour movement, many more wrongs have been righted by direct pressure than by the initiative of jurists or the good will of the powerful. Direct action may be about to enter a new field and bear its part in developing international justice. It is certainly one of the rights of citizenship, the hardest to exercise and the most liable to abuse, but inalienable.[1]

In considering these enduring problems of power and of the State, one must always bear in mind the close correspondence between political forms and their underlying social contents. The Marxist criticism of formal democracy is on the whole unanswerable: many of the rights that the liberal State grants to its citizens are abrogated by the facts of their economic and social existence. The parliamentary machine of the State is already little more than a survival: its wheels are revolving in a void; its orators sow the wind and reap the whirlwind. Political democracy needs to be wholly reorganized in relation to an effectual economic democracy adapted to the contemporary systems of production.[2]

Only upon this organic basis can the legitimate authority of the State be restored. To propose its restoration without saying by whom or with what ends in view, is merely to demand greater executive powers for established injustice. Ought the State then to disappear? Will the government of men be

[1] In reference to strikes, see special numbers of *Esprit: Grève et arbitrage,* July 1938; *La Grève est-elle anachronique?* March 1948
[2] *Y a-t-il deux démocracies? Esprit,* March 1946

one day replaced by the administration of things? One may well doubt this, since men and things are inextricably involved and it becomes more and more impossible to leave affairs to their own drift. And what State could conceivably renounce its own unity? Advocates of personalism have sometimes felt that their aspiration ought to be expressed by a demand for a 'pluralist State',[1] in which the division and balance of its constituent powers would mutually guarantee them against abuse. But the formula is in danger of appearing too contradictory; one should speak rather of a State articulated in the service of a pluralist society.

The education of the person

The development of the person in man, and the orientation of man towards the individual and collective requirements of the personal universe, begin from birth.

Our education has been described as a 'massacre of the innocents' on the largest scale.[2] Misunderstanding the person in the child, it imposes upon his mind a synopsis of adult conceptions of life including a scale of social inequalities, and replaces his own discrimination between characters and vocations by an authoritarian formulation of knowledge. The new educational movement, which is a reaction against this, has been partly misguided by liberal optimism, with its exclusive ideal of the thriving, philanthropic and well-adapted man. It needs to be reformed, one might say made more virile, by bringing it into the full perspective of individual and social man.

How is a child's education actually effected? The question depends upon another—what is its aim? Not to *make*, but to *awaken* personality. By definition, personality awakens itself

[1] *Esprit*, March, August-September, 1935

[2] JACQUES LEFRANCQ in *Esprit*. See also B. CHARBONNEAU: *La Fabrication des bons élèves, Esprit*, Nov. 1937, and the studies of Roger Gal in the same review.

in response to an appeal, and cannot be fabricated from without. The purpose of education cannot therefore be to fashion the child in conformity with an environment, either familial, social or of the State, nor can it be restricted to adapting the child to the function or occupation that he is to fulfil as an adult. The transcendence of the person means that the person belongs to nobody else but to himself: the child is a subject, it is not a *RES societatis* nor a *RES familiae* nor a *RES Ecclesiae*. Not that it is purely subjective nor an isolated subject. Inserted into various collectivities the child is educated by them and within them; if they are not all-powerful in its eyes, they are its natural formative environments—the family and the nation and (the Christian adds) the Church, are all avenues that open out towards a wider humanity.

The educational question cannot be reduced to the problems of the school: the school is only one educational instrument among others; and even to make it the principal instrument is a dangerous error. The school is not charged with the duty of imparting 'instruction' in the abstract, but with scholarly education, which is but one sector of the whole. This kind of education being that which is most closely linked with the needs of the nation—the formation of the citizen and the producer—is that which the nation, represented by its administrative organs, has the most direct right to supervise and organize. Schools are not organs of the State, but in our modern countries they are national institutions and their methods have to be shaped in accordance with the needs and the concrete situation of the nation, within the frame of natural educational rights. These conditions may sometimes require the dispersal, and at other times the concentration, of scholastic institutions, but never justify their becoming organs of the State. And the extra-scholastic areas of education ought to be allowed as complete freedom as possible.[1] Finally, considered as a function of the nation as a whole, school education should be open to all, none of its higher degrees being reserved for a privileged section of the people. Its function is to impart to everyone the minimum of knowledge that the free person requires, but also to call forth, from whatever social environment, those individuals of talent who, given effectively equal opportunity, will be able to discharge the directive responsibilities of the nation for each new generation.[2]

Culture

Culture is not one sector, but a comprehensive function, of the personal life. For a being who finds himself, and forms himself by a process of development, everything is culture, the management of a factory or the formation of a body no less than the conduct of a conversation or the cultivation of the soil. This is to say that there is not *a* culture, in distinction from which every other activity is uncultured (a 'cultured man') but there are as many kinds of culture as of activity. This point needs to be remembered against our bookish civilization.[3]

Since the personal life is that of freedom and self-surpassing, not of accumulation and repetition, culture does not consist, in any of its domains, in the heaping-up of knowledge, but in a deep transformation of the subject, enabling him to fulfil ever new possibilities in response to ever-renewed calls from

[1] For problems of education and of the school: Manifeste au service du personnalisme 98s. *Esprit*, Feb. 1936 (Pour un Statut pluraliste de l'école); Dec. 1944 (H. MARROU: *Protoschéma d'un plan de réforme universitaire*); March 1945 (ANDRE PHILIP: *Projet d'un statut du service public de l' enseignement*); March-April 1949 (Special number: *Propositions de paix scholaire*); Oct. 1949 (the same continued). A study that is still up-to-date is the *Theorie de l'education* of LABERTHONNIERE (Vrin).

[2] See the studies of JEAN GADOFFRE etc., studies published in *Esprit* in 1945, and reprinted in *Le Style du XX Siècle*. (Ed. du Seuil).

[3] See DENIS DE ROUGEMONT: *Penser avec les mains* (Albin Michel).

within. As someone has said, culture is that which remains when one no longer knows anything,—it is what the man himself has become.

It follows that, like everything else that is personal, culture is an awakening, it cannot be contrived or imposed. But neither can it develop, any more than anything else of a personal nature, in absolute liberty; or without being under pressure from a thousand solicitations and constraints which it finally turns to good account. Inventive even in its decline, culture elaborates orthodoxies and finally perishes under their tyranny. It is obvious that any culture, at a certain level of achievement, can and needs to be directed or, it would be better to say, sustained. But it will not endure being planned. And in its creative phases, it needs to go its own way alone, though in a loneliness freely responsive to every vibration of the great world without.[1]

Some degree of support from the collective life is indispensable to the creations of culture; when it is vital they can flourish, when it is mediocre they are enfeebled. Yet the creative impulse always acts through the single person, though he may afterwards be lost in the crowd; every folk-song had its first original composer: and even were all men to become artists, there would not be one art, but as many varieties of art as there were men. All that is true in the collectivist doctrine of culture is that any one class tends to imprison culture in conventions, and that the inexhaustible resources of cultural renewal are in the people themselves.

Once again—all culture is a transcendence and a renewal. As soon as a cultural development is arrested, it becomes anti-cultural—academic, pedantic or commonplace: as soon as it loses its sense of the universal it begins to dry up into specialisms. And as soon as it confuses universality with a static notion of totality, it hardens into a system.

[1] *Esprit*, special number: *Alerte à la culture dirigée*, Nov. 1936; *Trois Vues sur l'affaire Lysenko*, Dec. 1948

Most of these conditions obtain, more or less unrecognized, in the culture of today; hence its disorder. The social cleavage between the horny-handed and the white-collared, and prejudiced ideas about the priority of 'the spiritual' lead people to confound culture with book-knowledge and technology. The deep class divisions that accompany this prejudice have imprisoned culture, or at least its means, its privileges and sometimes its illusions, within a minority, to its sophistication and impoverishment. Here, one social class subjects culture more and more to its own ends; there, a government does the same; everywhere it is abused. As a common term between a society and its spiritual life, it is submerged by conventions on one side and the latest fashions on the other. Creative artists have no longer a public, and where a public exists they lack the means to make an appearance. Economic and social conditions are largely responsible for these privations; they produce a cultural caste which seduces art (of the court, the salon or the church) into esotericism, snobbery or preciosity to flatter its importance; into academicism for its reassurance; into frivolity for its distraction; and into pungency, complexity or brutality to relieve its boredom. As technique widens the choice of means and multiplies the possibilities of artistic production, the products are commercialized and cheapened to the greater profit of the smaller number, to the detriment alike of the producer, the work and the public taste. The condition of the artist, the professional and the man of learning thus oscillates between the poverty of neglect and the servility of a tradesman.[1] Many are the maladies so bound up with our social structure that its disappearance is the first condition for their cure. We must not therefore ignore two no less considerable factors in the enfeeblement of our culture: the bewilderment of the contemporary conscience, from which the vision of the great hierarchies of value (both religious and rationalist) are fading away; and

[1] See *Esprit*, special number: *L'Art et la révolution spirituelle*, Oct. 1934, and *Pour un nouvel humanisme*, Oct. 1935

the present obsession by mechanical and utilitarian ideas.

The position of Christianity

We sought to distinguish, in actual religious life, between the eternal reality, its expressions in temporal and perishable forms, and the compromises to which men reduce them. The religious spirit does not consist in the justification of all these together by apologetics, but in separating the authentic from the inauthentic, what will endure from what is obsolete. And here it makes contact with the spirit of personalism.[1]

The compromises of contemporary Christianity include several movements that are historical revivals. There is the old theocratic temptation of state-control of the conscience; the sentimental conservatism which would link the defence of the faith with that of out-of-date class-systems; and a stubborn logic of money that would over-ride the interests it ought to serve. Elsewhere, in reaction against these nostalgias and survivals, there are frivolous attempts to curry favour with the latest ideological success. Whoever wishes to maintain Christian values in their vigour should rather seek, by all means, to separate Christianity from these established disorders.

But that, after all, is but a very external activity in relation to the crucial problem that this age presents to Christianity. Christianity no longer holds the field. There are other massive realities; undeniable values are emerging apparently without its help, arousing moral forces, heroisms and even kinds of saintliness. It does not seem, for its own part, able to combine with the modern world (with its consciousness, reason, science, technology, and its labouring masses) in a marriage such as it

---

[1] See, especially, the numbers of *Esprit* on *Rupture de l'ordre chrétien et du désordre établi,* March 1933; *Argent et religion,* Oct. 1934; *Pour une nouvelle chértienté,* Oct. 1935; *Monde chrétien, monde moderne,* Aug.-Sept. 1946; also P. H. Simon, *Les Catholiques, la politique et l'argent* (Ed. Montaigne, 1935). The publications *Jeunesse de l'Eglise* devote permanent study to these problems.

consummated with the mediaeval world. Is it, indeed, approaching its end, of which this divorce is the sign? A deeper study of the facts leads us to believe that this crisis is not the end of Christianity, but only of a kind of Christianity. Perhaps the decomposing hulk of a world that Christianity built, that has now slipped its moorings, is drifting away, and leaving behind it the pioneers of a new Christianity. Or it would seem that, having for many centuries flirted, as it were, with the Jewish temptation, of trying directly to establish the Kingdom of God upon the plane of terrestrial power, Christianity is slowly returning to its first position; renouncing government upon earth and the outward appearances of sanctification to achieve the unique work of the Church, the community of Christians in the Christ, mingled among all men in the secular work,—neither theocracy nor liberalism, but a return to the double rigours of transcendence and incarnation. Nevertheless one cannot say that the tendencies of today, any more than those of yesterday, give final definition to the relations between Christianity and the world, because no such definition is possible. What is essential to each, is that the living spirit should be fostered.

The crisis of Christianity is not only a historic crisis of the Church, it is a crisis of religious values throughout the white man's world. The philosophy of the Enlightenment believed that religious values were artificially maintained, and was persuaded that they would shortly disappear. For some time this illusion could be kept up upon the rising tide of scientific enthusiasm. But if one sure conclusion can already be drawn from the experiences of this twentieth century, it is that as fast as these values in Christian vestments disappear, they reappear under other, more obsessive images: the body is divinised, or the collectivity, or the evolutionary striving of the species; or the Leader, or the Party, and so forth. All the regulative ideals that are set forth in the 'phenomenology' of religion come back again in novel cults and in generally debased forms, decidedly retrograde in comparison with those of Christianity, precisely because the personal universe and its requirements are eliminated.

The positions indicated in these few pages are debatable and subject to revision. For these are not conclusions drawn from the application of a received ideology; they have the free, provisional character of a progressive disclosure of the human predicament in our time. It cannot but be the hope of every personalist that these positions will develop as discovery proceeds, until the word 'personalism' itself be one day forgotten, because there will no longer be any need to direct attention to what will have become the common and accepted knowledge of the situation of mankind.

INDEX

A

Abraham, 89

Absolute power, 112

Abstention, spiritual malady of contemporary mind, 64

Action, 83–94; as existence, 83; presupposes freedom, 83; value of, 84; refusal of, 85, 91; classical distinctions, 86–94; prophetic action, 89; integral action 94; see also Blondel, M., on the dialectic of spirit and action, xix

Aero-dynamics, 105

Aeroplane, 105

Aesthetic of personalism, 77–79

Affirmation, the person in acting and choosing, 50–51; G. Marcel on, 66

Alternation, malady of contemporary mind, 64

Appropriation to disappropriation, 38–40

Art, 77–79; as affected by economic and social conditions, 120; as commercialised by developing technique, 120; contemporary art as symptomatic of nihilism, 78; failure of art a frustration of values, 81

Ascetic of self-dispossession, 21

Associated reflexes, of Pavlov, 5, 6

Atom, the, as embryonic personality, 7

Augustin, St., on transcendence, 65

Authenticity, 87

Averroes, xiii

B

Bakunin, conception of God, xiii; on freedom, 58

Behaviour, control of by biological and economic situation, 8

Bergson, Henri, xi; on the social impulse, 67

Bernanos, the free man, 52; on satisfied mediocrity, 99

de Biran, Maine, importance of his work, xvi

Blondel, Maurice, on dialectic of spirit and action, xix; on identity of existence and action, 83

Brave New World, ix

Body, the basis of consciousness and the spiritual life, 11; an obstacle to communication, 18

Bourgeoisie, founders of economic and spiritual individualism, xv

de Broglie, L., on pseudo-causality, 6

Brunschvig, Léon, 5, 73

C

Catastrophe, cult of, 100

Causality, principle of, and modern science, 55

Centralization, as condition of individualism, 19

Christianity, its notion of the person, xii–xiv; and Marxist teaching, 13; and personalism, 80, 81; position and crisis of, 121–123

INDEX

Feuerbach, Essays, 13

Force, 49, 50; Gandhi on rightful place of, 49

Ford, Henry, 12

Forgiveness as a liberating value, 22

Fortitude, Christian, 49

Freedom, nature of, 54–64; in relation to natural causes, 55, 56; modern science and, 55; of indifference, 54; in relation to the person, 58–63; falsifications of, 60–61; of choice, 63–64; as a unitive force, 64

French Revolution, as marking a phase of liberation, xvii

Freud, 9, 98

Frienfels, Müller-, 67

Frobenius, 30

Frustration, factors of, 83–85

Heidegger, 'One's world', 27; the 'inauthentic life', 33; love as a mutual disease, 17; on the value of refusal, 47, 48

History, 79–80; as a supreme value, 80

Hitler, 92

Holland, personalism in, xx

Howison, no reality behind personality, 65

Humanity, as one and indivisible, 30

Human nature, a conception rejected by contemporary thought, 29

Human phenomena to be explained by personalism, 9

Husserl, the intentional, part played by, 66

Huxley, Aldous, *Brave New World*, ix

G

Gandhi, as example of prophetic action, 89; on legitimate use of violence, 49

Generosity, function of, 22

Goethe, xvi

Good, the, a Person, 82

Greeks, their attitude to civilization, 87; sense of human dignity, xii

Gurvitch, G., on the emergence of the State, 112

H

Happiness, not the supreme value, 72

Hartmann, on 'values' as realities in themselves, 68

Hegel, as marking the end of philosophy, 99; on subservience of the individual to the State, xvi, xvii

I

Immortality, in Plato, xi

Impulse, the social, leading to closed societies, 66, 67

Incarnation, the, xiv; central importance of, in Christianity, 80, 89

Individual, the; Aristotle on, xii; opposed to 'the person', 19

Individualism, opposed to personalism, 17–19

Individuality, in the atom, 7; in the animal, 7

Industry, 13, 86

Instinct, of exteriorization (Klages), 44; of self-defence, 18

Intentional, the, a human reality, 66

Inter-subjectivity, conditions essential to, 28

Intimacy, 36–38; a concrete requirement of personality, 39

Irreducible, the, 51–53

INDEX

INDEX

Person, the—
   as transcending nature, 5; the transcendent in, 65; Renouvier on the nature of, xviii
Personal universe, the, 8, 9, 16, 76, 82
Personalism, History of the term, vii; in England, xx; in Holland, xx; in Switzerland, xx; in the U.S.A., xx
Personality, the atom as embryonic personality, 7; economic of, 22; expansion of, implies renunciation, 40; nature of, 45, 46; and the poetic life, 77
Personalization, of nature, 11–16; of values, 68–81; threatened by the technical age, 14
Personalization and depersonalization, 7
Plato, allegory of the cave, 74; on the individual soul, xi; on immortality, xi
Plurality of personalisms, viii
Politics, extent of, 111; as relating problems of economics and ethics, 86
Political parties responsible for political education, 114
Possession, dangers of, 40
Power, personalist doctrine of, 111–116; absolute, 112
'Primitive man', 8
Production, an essential activity of the person, 13; value of, 14
Progress, paralysed by war, 99
Property a concrete requirement of personality, 39
Prophetic Action, 89–90
Proudhon, xviii; on justice, 31; on love, 31; myth of imaginary society, 105
Pseudo-causality, de Broglie, L. on, 6

R

Radio-activity, and the new conception of matter, 7
Real, the, recognition of, first stage in creative life, 12
Religion, unable to live by pure spirit, 81; individualism of, opposed by Christian personalism, 81
Renaissance, call for a second, 99
Renouvier, on love, 31; on nature of 'person', xviii; first to use the term 'personalism', vii; no reality behind personality, 65
Revolution, the twentieth century, 97–123
Ricoeur, Paul, on philosophy of G. Marcel, 81
Rights, formal, insufficient safeguard, 28; value of legal, 28
Romanticism, xviii
Rousseau, on authority, 113; influence of, xvi

S

Sacrifice, the supreme act of the person, 66
Saint-Simon, 88
Salomon von, Ernst, 85
Sartre, 23, 47, 48, 56; 'being in itself', 56; discontinuity between free spirits, 30; freedom as a 'condemnation', 57; love as a mutual disease, 17; the person as producer akin to Marx's formula for man, 66; on 'self-deception', 33
Scheler, on 'Values' as realities in themselves, 68
School education, 117
Science as a value, 72; as condition of inter-subjectivity, 28; as ideal of last two centuries, 72;

INDEX

Science—

its importance to the ascent of the person, 73; its practical activities surpass its own definitions, 74

Self, as built up by choice, 63; in closed societies, 67; dependent on communication, 20; higher self, 33, 34; inmost self, 35, 36

Self-affirmation, as continual assimilation, 38

Self-commitment, theory of, 91–94

Self-dispossession the central ascetic of the personal life, 21

Self-recollection (the higher self), 33

Sexes, the relations of, 106–109

Silence, 34

Sin, ability to sin essential to full liberty, xiii; in relation to freedom, 76

Singular, the, 45, 46

Society, national and international, 109–111; inter-racial, 111; Western bourgeois, criticised, 18, 19

Societies, closed, a result of the social impulse, 67

Sorel, an inspiration to Lenin and Mussolini, 97

Soul, individual, Plato on, xi

Spinoza, 73, 83

Spirit, Christian doctrine of, 4

Stalin, 61

State, the, 111–116; rightful place of, 112; disappearance of, debated, 115; the Liberal State, xviii; pluralist state demanded, 116; necessary limitations of, 113

Suffering as a frustration of value, 81, 82; Spinoza, advice on, 83; Stoics, advice on, 83

Switzerland, personalism in, xx

Sympathy, an affinity of nature, 23; distinct from love, 23

Synthesis, dialectical, the logic of personalism, 75

Systematization, need for, viii

T

Technical age, the, a menace to personalization, 14; means to man's invasion of the universe, 14

Technique, modern, art as affected by, 120; freedom of decision, demand for, increased, 63

'Technique of spiritual procedure', research for, 84

Technocrat, the, 86

Thought, essentially communicable, 28

Totalitarianism, 32

Tragic optimism, the right road for man, 15, 16

Transcendence, Christianity the religion of, 80

Trinity, conception of the, xiv

Truth as a value, 73; not subjective, 74

Tyranny, origin in man not in things, 13

U

Unity, of the human being, xv; of the human race, xiv; of mankind, as leading idea of personalism, 30; of persons, 29–32; how obtained, 42; of the world, 110

Universe, of Malraux, 57; of Montherlant, 57; invasion of made possible by the technical age, 14; as a menace to man, 47

U.N.O., 110

United States of America, personalism in, xx

INDEX

V

Valéry, 43

Value, existing only as willed, 69, 70; always result of conflict, 71

Values, personalization of, 68–72; frustration of, 81, 82; pursuit of, inseparable from joy and suffering alike, 81; transcendence of, 75

Values of personalism; art, 77–79; happiness, 72; history, 79–80; moral values, 76; science, 72; truth, 73; religious values, 80, 81

Vertigo of the Abyss, 38

Violence not to be eliminated by history, 81

Vocation, doctrine of, 41, 42

W

War, and notion of non-intervention, 92; end-result of social disorganization, 99

Wave-mechanics, function compared to art, 78

World, the, and man, 9; 'One's world' (Heidegger), lowest level of consciousness, 27; of persons, 29; desperate condition of, today, 98, 99

World unity, 110

Z

Zola, E., *J'accuse*, 89